"The Power of You" is for anyone regardless of particular religious background interested in any of the following:

- Spiritual growth; how to rapidly expand awareness of our spirit selves
- A quicker, easier path to enlightenment/self-realization/God consciousness
- How to get the "gift" from suffering without the suffering; end the need for suffering
- Understand who and what God really is
- Specifically how and why we lost the awareness of who we are—God within us
- How to realistically conquer and surrender the ego
- How to achieve peace through challenging times; how to accept the unacceptable
- How to obtain Jesus' level of love, compassion and non-judgment
- Understand the real purpose we are in a physical reality here on earth
- Specific and practical step by step guidance through trying times
- How to effectively heal all pains from past experiences
- Know the cause of all illness and the only way prevent it
- How to experience peace, inner joy and true happiness to our highest capacity
- How to be a powerful creator and spontaneously manifest your desires
- How to rid yourself of guilt, resentment and shame
- Understand why we all feel "not good enough"
- Understand the one and only cause of all pain, separation and fear
- How to free yourself from the pattern of attracting unwanted experiences
- How to truly forgive yourself and others
- Recognize and overcome all hidden judgments and limitations
- Understand precisely how, when and why the ego was formed
- What happens when we die; where we go
- The real reason close relationships are the most challenging
- The truth about karma
- How to bring the power of God into you

THE POWER OF
YOU

*The End of Pain,
Separation,
and Fear*

CONNIE FOX

BALBOA.
PRESS

A DIVISION OF HAY HOUSE

Balboa Press books may be ordered through booksellers or by contacting:

Balboa Press
A Division of Hay House
1663 Liberty Drive
Bloomington, IN 47403
www.balboapress.com
1-(877) 407-4847

Because of the dynamic nature of the Internet, any web addresses or
links contained in this book may have changed since publication and
may no longer be valid. The views expressed in this work are solely those
of the author and do not necessarily reflect the views of the publisher,
and the publisher hereby disclaims any responsibility for them.

The author of this book does not dispense medical advice or prescribe the use
of any technique as a form of treatment for physical, emotional, or medical
problems without the advice of a physician, either directly or indirectly. The
intent of the author is only to offer information of a general nature to help
you in your quest for emotional and spiritual well-being. In the event you use
any of the information in this book for yourself, which is your constitutional
right, the author and the publisher assume no responsibility for your actions.

Any people depicted in stock imagery provided by Thinkstock are models,
and such images are being used for illustrative purposes only.
Certain stock imagery © Thinkstock.

Printed in the United States of America.

ISBN: 978-1-4525-8040-1 (sc)
ISBN: 978-1-4525-8041-8 (e)

Balboa Press rev. date: 11/8/2013

Table of Contents

Introduction

I am an American with roots in the Midwest and Florida. I suppose I have the typical background as an average woman of my generation with the usual interests and desires from the culture of my time.

As a young adult, I had some extraordinary experiences when I began communicating directly with spirit. This was spontaneous, unplanned, unasked for and greatly misunderstood by me. Little did I realize the value of tapping into this unlimited source of knowledge. Over the years I have learned how to implement this gift to my benefit as well as others. It is a great advantage to access knowledge beyond one's normal awareness.

I shared my communication gift by translating answers to other people's questions. At first, I worked with family and friends. It eventually advanced to consulting for clients, assisting them on a one-on-one basis with their personal or medical issues. I now communicate to and translate from the consciousness of cells within one's body, the spirit of animals, the deceased and most all other non-physical forms including Jesus.

For some time, Jesus has been asking me to share His messages to the world. I had been reluctant to do this mostly because of my fear of disapproval and rejection. First of all I work professionally in a scientific field as a Holistic Health Practitioner. Secondly, any sane person would not be entirely comfortable telling others she can communicate to anyone's spirit let alone the spirit of Jesus Christ. I know I'm no different or "higher" than anyone else. But I have grown to the point where I now have enough self-acceptance to be fully honest about who and what I am.

Jesus tells us how to deliberately expand spirit and heal all pains from past experiences. It's all about expanding spirit and healing your pain. Through His loving process you dissolve hidden judgments and limitations, freeing you to access the power of all that you truly are—the power of *You*.

Perhaps you think you are happy enough right now? Perhaps you feel you are already a loving person with enough inner peace and fulfillment? But if you are not fully aware of your true nature *beyond your mere physical reality*, you are not accessing the God-given power that is meant to be experienced. Jesus wants you to know there is so much more.

The second section of this book is from the prominent Mahavatar Babaji, the deceased spiritual teacher who resides deeply in my heart. I've kept this journal of our personal conversations in their original format from a time of challenging loss in my life. I went from a great life with excellent health and joyful expectations to a bed-ridden existence of hopelessness; from the lifestyle of multiple homes and a private jet to no home and living in a tent. I never intended to share these words with anyone ever. Our conversations are presented here because Babaji and Jesus urged me to do so. Anyone can read them and adapt them in a practical way to their own personal issues.

The third section of this book presents a variety of questions with answers from Jesus. The topics chosen came from family, friends and clients.

The last section shows how I "connected the dots" from these teachings, truly understanding how one can gain the power of God realization *now*—it need not take years, decades or multiple lifetimes to experience the full *Power of You*.

You may submit your own questions to me at my e-mail address: **Connie@AskConnie.biz** Your answers [names withheld] may appear on YouTube, my web site or a future book. Comments and suggestions are welcomed. Please visit me at: **www.AskConnie.Biz**

Connie Fox
February 14, 2013

Acknowledgments

My deepest love and gratitude to my mother, Susan Fox for being the most loving and devoted mother I ever could have been given. To my closest and dearest friend Mette Bergmann and her husband, Bent Breitenstein for your ongoing unconditional love and support as well as every single one of my clients. Without you, this book could not have been written.

Messages from Jesus

Message #1: Defining Jesus, God, One's Spirit Self and Ego

I would like everyone to understand exactly who and what I am. I ask you to relinquish and release all you have heard about me from your parents, teachers, churches, society, books and even the bible.

I, Jesus Christ, am not anything or anyone you may think I am. All I am is love, compassion and non-judgment. I am God's energy filled with nothing but love, compassion and non-judgment. That is all there is of any relevance about who and what I am. Nothing else matters. None of the stories you have heard, believe or do not believe, judge as accurate or inaccurate, matter not one bit. The only thing that is important to know about who I am is that I am nothing but love, compassion and non-judgment.

I *represent* love, compassion and non-judgment. When the bible says you must go through me, Jesus Christ, to reach heaven, to reach enlightenment, to reach God, to reach the Holy Spirit, to reach the Divine, to reach the full awareness of who your true self is, your undying self, your spirit self, your God self, or whatever you prefer to call it, you must go through *being* like me—all loving, all compassionate and all non-judgmental.

This is what I want to teach to whoever is desirous of listening: *how* to have all the love, compassion and non-judgment that I have. That is the first thing.

I would also like to explain what God is. God is not a being, physical or non-physical; not a form physical or non-physical, not a person, place or thing or even a spiritual being. God is a pure energy and is nothing but an energy that exists in every single atom of the universe.

This God energy is the source of all creation. I came to earth for the first time as a physical form of God's energy to bring the knowledge of love, compassion and non-judgment to all. People were not yet ready to let go of ego. This was and still is the fear of separation from God, the fear of feeling separate from God. You were not all quite ready yet. Still, the groundwork was laid.

Now, many of you on this planet are ready to be expanding spirit, your spirit self, at a much more rapid rate than ever before. I will be translated through Connie's communication gift to share with you that for which you are now ready. This is the transition from ego identity; the belief that you are separate from God and everyone else.

You will realize that God is who we really are—not separate, not fear, but pure God energy. Behind the ego's identity, behind the ego's fear of separation, is our true source, our true selves; our spirit self which is God's energy and my love, compassion and non-judgment as one.

This is who each and every one of you is already. The fact that you do not realize this, know this or feel this is simply because of lack of awareness. It is only your identification with ego that keeps you in ignorance of this truth. It keeps you in fear and in a state of separation from God and everyone and it does this always through the use of judgment.

Question: Would you please explain more about the ego? What is your definition of the ego?

The ego is the mind, basically. That is, the mind's perception comes from the ego. The ego is only able to perceive through the five physical senses—hearing, touch, sight, taste, smell. The ego cannot identify with anything beyond the five physical senses. Your spirit self can identify only with love, compassion and non-judgment.

Most people are born with the lack of awareness of their spirit self—their true self's level of awareness, which is nothing but love, compassion and non-judgment. Usually you have awareness only of your ego's identity. You are here to become more of your true self by making the transition from ego identification to full awareness of your spirit self.

The ego is formed by your life's experiences combined with how you judge them, all which is controlled by your ego's perception. There are several ways to develop yourself spiritually, to increase your level of awareness of spirit self, to develop your heart's full capacity of love and compassion without the ego's judgments.

Message#2: Judgment and How to Be Free of It

I am happy you are reading this because what I have to say next is my favorite topic of discussion. It is about judgment, the only thing that prevents one from fully loving themselves and others. It is the only thing that creates pain, separation and fear. When you become aware of how and when you judge, that alone is a big leap forward in developing your spirit self.

Remember when I said your spirit is God energy, which is pure love energy? This is now an ideal time for everyone on this planet to be given more clear advice, more specific direction about how to evolve spiritually. Spiritual evolution increases your ability to love yourself and others more fully.

Now, how do you become more aware of your judgments and then overcome them? Your judgments are what keep you in fear and separation. So let's understand further about what judgments are and how they continue to separate you from love.

Everyone feels "not good enough" in one way or another. Why do you all feel not good enough in some way? Because of the ultimate judgment from the ultimate separation that occurs at birth. At birth you lost the awareness that you *are* God. This is the meaning of "original sin".

One is born into a limited, restricted physical body and that act alone creates division. Imagine being your adult self as you are now. Able to walk, talk, move your body as you would like. Now imagine being put into a newborn infant's body. This would certainly be a frightening experience. You cannot talk, use your arms, walk or do anything for yourself. You are so restricted now in this infant's body that you are incapable of being who you really are.

One usually feels this limitation as the pain of birth and if you are not able to release that pain you will accept the ego into your mind. The moment you are born you have a split second to make a choice. Few are able to immediately accept that fearful experience of separation from God without judging it. You are now in a separate physical body in a separate physical existence. You now judge yourself as being separate—separate from God and from all things. Fear is now in your perception.

You are not in tune with what is beyond the physical. That is why you are here; to learn how to experience and express the love that you are into this physical world. This time on earth is ideal for evolving spiritually at a very quick rate. It is in perfect timing that I am able to share my messages to all who care to listen.

A lot of people are going around minute by minute, day to day, month to month, stuck in the same old pattern of judging and this situation has been stagnating for quite some time. Your time to grow is NOW.

Question: Will you please talk more about how and why everyone feels not good enough?

As I mentioned, you feel separation from God the moment you are born because you are born into a separated existence. In your physical world, there must be separation—separate people in separate physical bodies, separate places and things—it is not unified in a physical reality. So, you identify yourself as separate rather than unified. Not united with any, not united with God.

The "original sin" is that you judge this separation that everyone experiences the moment you are born, with fear. That is the original sin—fear of being separate from God; the not knowing who you really are—union and unity—oneness with all. It is perceived as if you turned your back on God.

But indeed, you did not turn your back on God and you could not. You just lost the awareness of God for a time. Yet you will always sense guilt and feel shame from this fear. You don't know why. You do not logically understand why. Yet there is an underlying feeling each of you have from the moment of your birth. This is called guilt and it comes from the fear of being separated from God.

It is this guilt which creates that feeling of "not being good enough". You continue to grow up feeling "not good enough" in a variety of ways. You learn from your parents, family, churches, friends, society, schools and teachers how they feel they are not good enough also. You learn what is considered good enough and what is considered not good enough. It is all just a matter of incorrect perception. You absorb and learn all sorts of judgments from the moment you are born and all throughout your life. If you are reading this now, it is time to learn how to replace these illusions about yourself and others. Whatever you believe about yourself you will also find ways to believe about others. When you judge yourself or another for any reason whatsoever, know that it is merely a manifestation of your own fear. For now, just acknowledge that as much as you can.

An example I've used before when discussing this with Connie, is of a young child playing with a toy when another child comes along, sees the toy and grabs it. The first child gets upset and starts crying. If you witnessed this event you would automatically understand that the child who grabbed the toy simply does not know any better. Although you may try to teach the child kind and appropriate behavior, you would not judge that child harshly for not yet knowing better behavior.

That is how I see anything and everything—any form of action with anyone—with the understanding that you have not yet learned better. Maybe this can help you apply understanding to any situation that causes you to form a judgment.

When someone or something bothers you, hurts you, upsets you, angers you or disappoints you, and this goes for yourself too—forgive yourself for not yet being fully aware of who you are. Likewise, forgive others.

All of you are here to learn how to love to your highest capacity while still in a physical body. Have compassion for this process that you and all others are going through. Choose understanding, compassion and forgiveness.

Question: You talked about not feeling good enough because when we are born we lose the awareness of God. Is that why we always feel as if something is missing and we start looking outside ourselves for something or someone else to fill that empty void?

Yes. This is where the ego starts chasing you or you start looking for something that can make you feel happy as you try to fill the void or underlying emptiness that is ever present. Since you are now only aware of your limited ego-self, you search for things, situations or people in the physical world. You may feel you never have enough—enough money, or 'enough' of a partner, enough status, or your house or car isn't 'enough', so you need a bigger, better house, more clothes and the list could go on.

But I want to clear a common misunderstanding. You are here to experience the highest, most desirous, most pleasurable experiences you can. You are here to enjoy life to the fullest in the material world, which of course includes material things. That is why you are here.

Your spirit is always yearning to expand so that you may become more aware of it. Yet, you cannot be filled with love from things or from believing certain things such as being pretty enough, smart enough, rich enough, tall enough, thin enough, etc. This does not mean material qualities are not to be experienced and appreciated. Only this: do not get stuck in the pattern of thinking that only certain things, people or situations outside of yourself are any solution for true happiness and inner peace. Nothing outside of yourself can satisfy that feeling inside of you that is seeking God.

Enjoy the many outer things in your physical life, while knowing they will not replace the feeling inside of you that impels you to seek God.

Message #3: How Do We Create True Happiness and Peace?

Do you desire everlasting happiness and fulfillment? To remove the guilt, the emptiness, the sorrow that is always present within you? It is not because you are bad. It is not because you deserve less than experiencing the fullness of who you really are. It is because you are not aware of who you really are—your spirit self—God.

When you grow spiritually your ego remains as always. But, you start to realize you are not *only* your ego's perception, you are not *only* a physical body in a physical world where everything is separate from everything else. You begin to change from fear based perception to love based perception. It is this spiritual growth which is needed to achieve everlasting peace, happiness, fulfillment and inner joy beyond your wildest imaginings. Love and loving so fully, it is hard to imagine.

The way to obtain lasting peace is to become peaceful. How do you become peaceful? Through being happy. And how do you achieve being happy? There are a variety of answers to this question, the first and foremost being: *you come into alignment with your spirit.*

Now I'd like to discuss how to come into alignment with your spirit more rapidly.

First, you must have the desire to do so.
Then you develop your spirit by expanding it.

There are a variety of ways to develop spiritual expansion.

One way to expand spirit is:

By being fully present in each moment. This means your mind is fully present right along with you and what you are doing in each moment. Judgment of the past brings regret and resentments. Judgment of the future creates worry.

Of course you will use your logical thinking mind as needed to learn from past experiences and to plan effectively for your future. But, do not dwell in the past or future, live in the present moment. Being fully present in the moment allows escape from the ego; it releases the ego. Ego is always present no matter what, but you are not associated with it or attached to it when your attention is fully in the present moment. Then, it cannot cause you emotional pain and suffering—the sorrow, the anger, the guilt and the fear.

When fully present in the moment, you put the ego aside. It is still there, but you do not give it credence; you do not feed it your attention. Being in the present moment is always the ultimate of all that will bring one to self, to spirit self—peace, love and harmony at all times.

Cosmic habit-force is what ties you to your old ways of thinking. It is a hard thing to let go of when you are not used to it. It is not even possible without first expanding spirit and that requires healing the heart, healing the pain in the heart. Both expanded spirit and a healed heart are required for enlightenment—the full power of God, the full power of You. Your experience of life is then so beautiful, filled with so much gratitude, so much beauty, so much love and so much inner joy. There are no words to describe it. No words could describe it without limiting it greatly.

Having a healed heart means you are capable of *containing* more love, more compassion and non-judgment. This is where "Babaji's Work" comes in [section 2 of this book]. He teaches how to effectively heal all hidden pain in your heart.

Another way to expand spirit is to:

Meditate daily. Find a meditation that you feel good about; one you are comfortable with and that effectively stills the mind's thoughts. Stilling the mind's thoughts connects you to Source, your true self automatically. When you have a still mind, a mind that is not racing with lots of thoughts, you are able to connect to the God energy within.

Another way to expand spirit is to:

Love. Find a way to love. Take some initiative and be alert to the opportunities that surround you. Love who you are, what you do, others and all that is around you.

If you have millions of dollars in the bank but do not spend it, you will live like a pauper; you will not experience the wealth or the joys that come with it.

Bringing love into your life is possible only by first giving it away, by extending love outward. The best way to love yourself and others more is to give acts of love and kindness to yourself and others in any way you can.

Another way to expand spirit is:

Acknowledge all uncomfortable emotions. Allow yourself to feel unwanted emotions. In time you will experience these feelings as they arrive without judging them as "bad" or as unwanted.

Ego is a part of you as much as your spirit self. You cannot will or wish the ego away. No matter how wonderful your life is or is not, negative emotions will always come and go. Allow them to come, honor their presence when they come. Do not attempt to ignore them. Do not judge them as being unwanted or bad or yourself as being bad because you have those feelings. Do not judge others for having their negative emotions either. Honor them all and their power will become nil.

Ego will always find a way to express the lack of union it feels about not being Spirit; about not being God, because it is not. Ego will always feel separate, inferior, sad, angry, offended, or worried. The ego is everything that spirit is not.

Question: Please further explain "honor them" when referring to negative emotions.

Validate them by giving them your attention. Respect your feelings. Respect yourself having those feelings. Validate them as being authentic.

When negative emotions are strongly felt, give yourself time alone to honor them. Feel them without judgment or blame. Allow yourself to recognize and identify the feeling. Is it worry, anger, sadness, frustration, etc.? Allow yourself to feel it fully so you do not accumulate even more suppressed emotional pain.

Question: Why? What good comes out of sitting there just concentrating on feeling strong, painful emotions? Can't that cause you to strengthen your anger into uncontrollable rage? Won't that turn sadness into a black hole of severe depression? Why try to feel more pain?

First of all, it is the resisting of emotions, the non-acceptance of them which make them painful. When such emotions are ignored they actually intensify but in a way that buries them beyond your recognition. Eventually these shunned emotions will surface—perhaps explosively and uncontrollably; or perhaps gradually as a diminished passion for life, inner joy and happiness. In time they will manifest into a physical imbalance or illness.

So clearly identify and honor all your emotions as they arise, dealing with them at that time. If circumstances prevent you from doing this immediately, please create the space and time to do so as soon as possible. Do Babaji's Work.

Another way to expand spirit is:

Through prayer. Ask for the expansion of your spirit from who you honor and revere as your God. Communicate to God, pray to God. When you pray you are feeling. What you are feeling when you pray is most important. Prayer has become misunderstood and I want to talk about it now.

Prayer is to promote feelings of gratitude and love and all the happiness that goes with it. It is intended to strengthen and promote more good, more appreciation, more happiness, more fulfillment and more love.

When you pray for help, pray with gratitude and desire for help. Do not ask with desperate feelings of despair, for that further disconnects you from God. Do not involve fear or despair with praying. It is not ideal to have these feelings with connecting to God. This is because it strengthens your feelings of being weak and small while you see God as being strong and powerful— and separate from you. Ask for what you want or need help with, but ask with gratitude, not with feelings of pain and separation.

The reason prayers work is because your desires are meant to be fulfilled when they are in alignment with your spirit self. This is how prayer works. Your desires literally move creation energy, God energy. Your desires are waiting to be fulfilled automatically. The energy of the universe is constantly moving from everyone's desires and if everyone's desires were in harmony with their spirit selves there would be instant heaven on earth.

Question: I think you are saying prayer is not meant to be desperate cries for help. But I think there are times in everyone's life that we do cry out to God in despair.

Yes. When you are in despair so deeply you are crying out to God for help. Yes, yes, yes. But when you are doing your regular daily praying, do it with feelings of gratitude, happiness and making clear your desires to God. During those most challenging times, yes of course. Seek God's help from a place of challenge. That is fine.

Another Way to expand spirit is:

Be effective at receiving good things; good relationships, good experiences and material items. Appreciate and value receiving without guilt, without shame and without feeling unworthy. Feel great about receiving everything good—good relationships, good food, good life, good everything.

Another way to expand spirit is:

Be in nature. Be in and surrounded by nature or a "nature-like" environment when you can. Many varieties of life forces are found in a natural environment; water, plant life, birds and other animal life. They typically contain peaceful energies, not stressful energies. Trees in particular instill peace.

Another way to expand spirit is:

Refrain from judging yourself and others. See all with compassion, understanding and forgiveness as you would if observing a young child who simply doesn't know better. That is all there is to that. Do not judge yourself or others negatively for not yet knowing how to do better.

Another way to expand spirit is:

Discover your joy. Discover your passions. Your purpose should be that which makes you excited and are passionate about. This greatly promotes happiness and being happy expands spirit.

If you need help in finding your passions, you must first get a few things out of your trained mind. There is nothing practical about your purpose. What makes you excited? For most people there will be many things. Write them down and use your logical thinking mind to figure out the steps needed to implement them into your life. That is a good general guideline.

Whatever makes you the most excited and joyfully exhilarated, do it. Make it a priority in your life to spend time doing that which you love and are naturally passionate about.

Another way to expand spirit is:

To save a life. Save an animal, a person, any living being, a tree or a plant. Save a life.

Of course saving a human life might bring more significance to you, but it is the act and the intent behind it that matters; the love and the caring. That could be given as much to a tree as to a person.

Message #4: A Simple New Recommendation to Promote Awareness of Spirit

Visualize God and yourself united as one. Are you ready to take evolving spiritually another step higher? Now for some new information that has not been said before. A new time it is and you are ready for this new knowledge.

When you pray, imagine seeing a light above your body. See a big bright light in front of you and above you. That bright light is God energy. Powerful, loving, beautiful energy that is capable of hearing your prayer, capable of seeing you there, praying. It is an energy that is the source of all creation and it is in every atom of the universe including your own body and your own being.

Acknowledge that this big light in front of you and above you, at this moment is God energy. Know this huge, bright and powerful light is also inside of you; inside every single cell of your body. This simple, brief intentional vision will begin to connect the hidden dots in your mind that you are not separate from God.

This creates the assumption that God is not separate from you. God is within you. When you pray to God you are also praying to your spirit self. They are one and the same. This will help you begin to fill a disconnection there, to fill a missing gap, to acknowledge that you are not separate from God, your Source. Your Source is within you.

Sounds very simple and it is. This will change your limited mindset, your limited understanding. Your heart will expand in ways that can only be understood through experience. It promotes the ridding of separation, the ridding of fear.

Message #5: The Importance of Mothers and Fathers

Mothers and fathers would do best to raise their children with their God-given expertise. Notice you have lost the appreciation for what each role plays in your society and I want to discuss this because it is important.

Mothers need to be more available when raising children. Fathers need to be more available when raising children. Children are often missing special qualities from each parent and it is changing society in a harmful way. This needs to be recognized.

Mothers need to be able to nurture their children from birth on throughout their childhood. This is not to say they are to handle everything. They do best with support from family, friends and community.

Parenting is not meant to be one-on-one only; one-on-one with all, one-on-one with a child. You are naturally meant to work together in families, neighborhoods, society—with friends, family and all. Your nature is not as a loner or couples as loners either. The lack of working in a connected manner with friends, family and community creates a more unnatural separation. This unnatural separation creates a generation of like and then another generation of like; continually creating more separation, more *not* connecting.

You are each not supposed to be doing everything—working in and out of the home, perhaps overwhelmed with the raising of children—and so it is the same for fathers. Fathers are just as important and needed to impart their area of expertise. Yes, they nurture also, but are needed for their own type of strength, courage, direction and feelings of security.

Mothers need to share their heart qualities; caring, sharing, loving, giving, kindness, working together. Each—mothers and fathers—have all qualities, but in a different way. You already know how different men and women are. This does not mean that you need to be conforming to specifically assigned roles.

There is no higher, bigger or better for either. They just have their own influence.

Neither mothers nor fathers seem able to have the time, attention or energy to naturally impart their qualities to the raising of their children. Parents are too busy and too stressed. The society will not come together in a complementary way for all if this value system is not being promoted.

Question: Do we not all have both male and female aspects? And, as we evolve won't they become more balanced also?

Yes. Everything becomes more balanced. All loving qualities become heightened and more balanced, but there are always going to be differences in your make-up. And they complement each other perfectly. Each needs the other to be well balanced. This is where great imbalance is a crime. Children are not getting both in a balanced way. There is a reason that is takes a man and a woman to conceive a baby. You need to honor and acknowledge the importance that each give to the child which creates your society. This awareness has been lost.

Question: What about gay relationships and their adoption of children?

There is still a male and female role with gay couples. One has more male qualities and one has more female qualities.

Message #6: The importance of living a balanced life

You must learn how to release stress. When you become unhappy enough, exhausted enough, and stressed enough, you will be ready for this message.

The easiest, simplest and most effective way to release stress is to meditate daily. It gives you the support you need through connecting to Source. It is the silence within that most are unaware of because the mind is too busy, too active, too distracted.

Use the type of meditation that feels best to you. Ask yourself: does it help you get in touch with the stillness within you? Does it effectively still your thoughts, calm you, make you feel more peaceful and more energized? Choose accordingly.

Prioritize your time. Prioritize financially as needed. Prioritize your joy. You and your partner or family if you have one, needs to establish a comfort zone. Establish what goals will help you to create a more balanced life and write them down even. It will be different for everyone. It could mean moving to a different location, selling your home or car for a more affordable one, so you can live a more balanced life. You may need to limit shopping. What you need to do is create the situation of more of your time being spent according to that which most feels good; that which brings you the most happiness and joy. An automatic way of un-stressing is by doing that which you love. Every day, spend time doing that which you enjoy.

Set priorities to allow for your eight hours of sleep every night and the time needed to eat three healthy meals in an enjoyable fashion. *A balanced life.* You need to make it clear to yourself what that is and what it takes to make changes that enable you to be more balanced with your time and resources.

Question: Some people cannot cut back or restructure their lives in a positive way. They have too much work, too little time

and they live an unhealthy, unbalanced life just to keep a roof over their head. What do you recommend in this case?

Do what you can each day as your life presently is now. You *can* meditate daily. You *can* try to fit in a little more time doing that which you enjoy, even if for just a brief time. If you're not eating well, try to improve that by doing what you can manage in the present, as it is. Have the desire, the goal and the intention to balance your life.

Make specifically clear what you want. Do you want to be able to work less hours, or eat healthier meals, or rest more or whatever? Ask God for help and support. Meditate every day. This will bring in more support than anything. You are connecting to God when you meditate and you create more effectively when you connect with Source regularly.

Message #7: Develop Communities based on Living a Balanced Happy Life

Are you ready to change your lives and the lives of others? Are you ready for existence on earth to change from living in a fearful, separating, judgmental existence, to living in peace, joy, happiness, fulfillment, love and harmony with each other, harmony with oneself, harmony with nature, harmony with your God self? That would mean not living for and through the ego. It is time to grow. It is time to evolve spiritually.

So, what I want to discuss now, is the importance of creating goal oriented communities of people who deliberately choose to evolve spiritually, live healthy, harmonious lives and support one another in doing so.

I want to say now, this does not mean you separate yourselves from all others to form a clannish civilization that is based on separating yourselves from everyone else in the world who is different—no, no, no.

I refer to a community where everyone accepts everyone being their unique, individual selves; the acceptance of individuality. One need not focus on beliefs being different from others, race or culture, sex or religion. No, no, no. This is a community that does not care about those separating, labeling, judgmental egoic ways. *All* of existence would be honored.

It is a community where you all learn to live independently without the need of a government to provide for you and everyone helping everyone else in your community and those who want to spiritually evolve and achieve enlightenment, live a balanced life, a non-segregating, non-separating life. A community like this would be the first of its kind. It could be an example which other communities could follow. This would begin to grow like wild flowers, these communities.

Those who are open to expanding their spirit self are going to remain on this planet and create a new existence on earth—an existence that is filled with love, compassion and non-judgment. An existence filled with peace, harmony and serenity which will bring joy, fulfillment, true happiness and enlightenment. Those of you who are not open to expanding your spirit will instead be leaving this planet to continue evolving in another form.

I want to share certain recommendations to build and create an ideal community which will in turn, create other similar communities around the globe and create peace on earth at last—enlightenment for all.

The first thing I'd like to address is where these communities need to be located to be safe from what is coming to this planet in the next several years. This several year period has recently begun so that should let you know the importance of beginning the building of these communities as soon as possible.

I will need to address every country on earth. I will share this information through Connie in my following messages. In America, the ideal locations to build these communities are mostly in and near the more northern sections of the United States—the closer to the mountains, the better. I will give Connie more specifics on these locations later.

It is imperative that these communities be independent, able to have or produce what is needed for several years to survive on all levels; medical care, security and protection, equipment needed to build homes and buildings to accommodate all needs, all professions. For example, the community will need a few dentists, a few doctors, veterinarians, builders, teachers, farmers, laborers, mechanics, technicians, specialists in providing protection, etc. All need to have enough goods, clothing, tools, equipment and supplies that can last for several years. Survival needs would include ongoing food, water, and power source.

I want to emphasize the importance of food. There is a time coming when food will not be available at stores. In time you will need to provide your own food. Be conscientious about knowing this so you are well prepared. Being in colder climates, greenhouses will be critically important, as well as planting enough vegetation, fruit/nut trees, vegetables, herbs; having eggs, meat, dairy—whatever you want for food, know that you have to provide it for yourselves.

Create self-sustainable homes and a self-sustainable community. Neighbors can share or trade with each other. For example, a neighbor can share their eggs for your apples or their services for your services, but need no one outside of your community. Approximately two hundred people would be the ideal size for these communities. They should not have much more than three hundred people.

Question: Is modern technology going to be lost at some point?

Not lost, but many will have it unavailable for a period of time.

Question: What is going to create all this—modern technology being unavailable, food in stores unavailable, the need to have security and protection, etc.?

A war is coming Connie—the last war on earth. Chemical warfare will be used. This will create illnesses never seen or heard before. Some will be contagious. Being in a colder climate will help protect you from this. The air will be contaminated also. Being in colder climates will save people's lives from such environmental damage. Living closer to the mountains or certain locations near the ocean will be of great value. You will need to be able to protect yourselves and your community from hoarders willing to do anything to survive.

You may want to have a hub or town center for the community. Have what you want there—perhaps rooms for teaching, an exercise area, an activities area, a store that trades goods, professional offices or meeting rooms. There will not be money in this community. For a time, money will be obsolete world-wide.

There needs to be a "board of directors" for the community that will collaborate for how to structure the community. It will consist of people with the ability to financially support the building of this community, skilled and adept at running a business successfully and that are in alignment with the teachings in this book. In time, the American government will not exist as it is now. There will be no more government as we know it in any country and all people will live fully independently within their own communities.

Question: Why is a such a war coming if there are more people ready to spiritually evolve now than not? If that were so, I would think the circumstances on earth would continue to improve, not get worse.

I'll give you a simple answer. Destruction is sometimes necessary to improve something. The destruction coming to earth within the next several years is a result of increased collective consciousness. The people that have the ability to evolve to a higher level of consciousness need an existence that enables them to continue to grow. This war coming will remove people that are inhibiting others from continuing to evolve spiritually.

It will also enable spiritual evolution for the people that cannot continue to evolve on earth. These people will literally need a new location that will be able to provide what they need to continue evolving. It is the process of evolution. When all are enlightened on earth, there will never be a need for mass destruction again. There will never again be pain, separation and fear. It has taken a long time for people on earth to be willing to love enough to let go of ego. People become more desirous and willing to surrender their pain, separation and fear when they are experiencing it, not when they are unconsciously aware of it.

Question: Jesus, you must know that this information might instill fear in some people. Could you please comment on this?

Like it or not, you all have created this and ignoring it will not make it go away. All anyone needs to do to prevent the need to have a 'mass destruction' *in their personal lives* is to expand heart and spirit.

In my next messages through Connie, I will give more details for how to live in harmony with all, to evolve spiritually at a rapid rate and create a joyous life, peace and ultimate freedom—enlightenment—heaven on earth. There is no single ideal way for everyone, but somewhat optimal ways of spending your time, ways of learning, healing, eating, structure of your home life, working together in the community and a wide variety of other issues.

Thank you very much for reading my messages and participating.

Conversations with Babaji
A Quicker Path to Christ Consciousness

Conversations with Mahavatar Babaji: "Babaji's Work"

[I included a few brief conversations with Jesus and one other spiritual saint]

January 18, 2011

Babaji, were you born enlightened; self-realized?

No. I was born as you were. The only thing that enabled me to overcome the ego was to succumb to it.

How did you succumb to it?

I engulfed myself in its misery. I allowed it to be. I allowed it to be.

How did you allow it?

Be alone and feel the deepest pain in your heart and feel it fully. Feel it, nothing else. Try to feel it. When you grasp it, never let it go. And stay there until you are free. When you embrace it fully, you will find God.

So, you suggest I be alone and try to feel the deepest pain in my heart?

Yes. Feel it intently. Try not to ignore anything. Go deeper than the pain you feel and then go deeper again and spend time there and when you do, God will be underneath.

If you don't mind me asking, what was your deepest pain you had to feel?

I felt no other pain than the loss of God.

Can you tell me what the deepest pain is in my heart, so I can try to get in touch with it when I get alone and try doing this?

Yes. You are in pain for one reason only—feeling the loss of God.

So, you suggest I try to feel the place in my heart that feels pain from feeling separate from God?

Yes. Every other pain is a figment of your imagination.

Isn't feeling separate from God also a figment of our imagination?

Yes. It is the core beneath all other pain. It is under this pain that you will find God. Connie, tell me why you want to experience God again. You had some temporary experiences of Christ consciousness years ago.

Because it feels so wonderful; total bliss, total love, ecstatic love, ecstatic gratitude, beyond complete peace. I didn't have an ounce of fear about anything. I knew I was completely immortal. I felt total compassion and the most extreme opposite of loneliness. I was connected to and united with everyone and everything in my surrounding. I felt total completeness. It was beyond energizing and invigorating. I felt so amazing, so beautiful, so powerful, but totally humble at the same time; an awe-striking, overwhelming bliss, peace, pure love and gratitude.

Yes. Now think of that after you feel the deepest pain in your heart.

Anything else?

Yes. Call God to you deeply. Call for God deeply. Beg for God. Remember Connie, your ego has you fooled. Do not forget your ego has you fooled. Just know that.

Jan 19, 2011

Babaji, anything you want to say?

I can tell you how to get in touch with the deepest part of your pain.

Ok. How?

Be alone, be comfortable and think about what you are most distressed about. Then think about why you perceive that person, circumstance or issue as disturbing. Think of yourself, not the disturbing issue. Then take it one level deeper and ask again: why am I perceiving this as disturbing or painful? Get to the source of why. Realize the why is because of your perception, not because of the issue.

Then ask yourself how you would feel if God agreed with how you perceive this? You would feel justified, yes. Now what? The issue you are disturbed by is still the same, isn't it? Now let it go—your resistance to that issue. Accept it with gratitude. It is teaching you what you believe or feel you are not. You are going to have to face everything you feel you are not; until you honor it. Honor it graciously.

The issue that's bothering you is showing you the lack you feel that is not really there. When the center of the issue is discovered and accepted, it disappears. All of your issues will come and go until they are discovered and honored. When you've reached them all and there are no more false perceptions of lack, you become one with all the issues and devour them away.

Then you have only love left in your heart and God never delays for a second, a heart that is full of nothing but love. Forgive everyone, every circumstance for being the mirror you need to love yourself fully.

Babaji, why am I feeling so drawn to you? So pulled to you? It is strange. I just found out who you were yesterday. I don't even know you!

Yes Connie, I am your father now.

What do you mean by that?

I am your teacher now.

I wish you were still here in a physical body so I could really be with you.

I am with you now more than physical nearness.

How can that be?

Because it is the heart that binds us closely, not physical nearness.

Can you tell me anything more about your personal experience during your transition from ego identity to enlightenment; Christ consciousness; God awareness?

Yes, Connie. I am happy to share this beginning with you. Connie, I was full of ego—not even close to God consciousness. There was one thing that helped me more than anything else. It was being given a devotee of Christ as I am for you. Christ consciousness is me. It is beyond your deepest imaginings. It is so beautiful and filled with so much gratitude to have Christ consciousness. Christ heals. And anyone with Christ consciousness is destined to be a healer. You, Connie are going to experience Christ consciousness sooner than you think. You are going to be a healer.

Really?! How? Why?

Because you need to.

That answer wows me!

Yes. I know it does. Soon it will be second nature to you.

I barely know what to say right now.

Say nothing and feel my love for Christ and you. It will grow in you as you feel it in me. Just feel me. Say nothing.

What did your devotee of Christ, your spiritual teacher teach you?

He taught me how to love and surrender to God.

How did he teach you that?

He withered away my ego as I am now with you.

What can I do or not do to help you with this, to help progress this process?

Feel my love. There is no quicker way. Listen to my mantra (om namah shivaya) and pour your heart out to Christ. There is no other way.

Don't I love and pour my heart out to Jesus already?

Yes. Do it deeper. Do it more. Do it deeper. Do it more. Christ is waiting Connie. I will get you there as my teacher did me.

So, your mantra is an ideal mantra to use when meditating?

No. It is not to be used as a mantra during meditation. It is not a mantra that is intended to help one still the minds thoughts and connect to God, the silence within. It is a mantra that induces healing the heart.

Hmmm. That's interesting. Ok. So, I should just listen to a song that sings your mantra or say it out loud or repeat it silently sometimes, in my head?

Yes, exactly.

I've been watching this you tube video, titled, "Teachings of Babaji" over and over displaying photos of you and your teachings as it plays a song that repeats your mantra. It said that whoever says your name in reverence receives an instant spiritual blessing. Is this literally true? And if so, what does receiving a blessing from you really mean?

Yes, Connie. I am no where you are not.

What does that mean?

I am everywhere now as Christ is. When someone is ready to let go of ego, I will be there. I will take them to our beloved Christ. That's the blessing.

Jesus, I know this may be a silly question, but are you sure you don't feel a little slighted or neglected that I've been speaking to Babaji more than you in the last few days?

Connie, I am Babaji. Babaji became one with me already.

I don't know what else to say right now.

Feel your love and devotion to me and Babaji.

Before I go for now, do you Jesus or Babaji have anything you'd like to say?

Follow Babaji and you follow me.

Jesus, some people that have a specific religion, sometimes prefer to have a spiritual teacher that is of their own religion. Since Babaji was eastern Indian and I'm presuming a Hindu, are there other spiritual teachers that can help lead one to you and God, but of their own religion?

Connie, there are many. One clear way of being able to determine if a spiritual teacher is capable of leading one to me and God is to acknowledge if they have all love, all compassion and all non-judgment. If not, find another spiritual teacher.

Many religions seem to have a lot of judgments or rules based on judgments. Many feel it is bad, wrong or unacceptable to get divorced, to commit adultery, to be gay, to have an abortion, drink alcohol, gamble, kill or harm another, not attending church regularly, etc. What about religions that have some rules and judgments like these?

Some of these practices of living are helpful to increasing your level of self-love. But any group, religion or organization that feels judgment toward anyone that performs any of these actions or any other action, is not being all loving, all compassionate and without judgment. Where there is judgment, there is separation. Separation always leads to self-suffering. Separation will never bring you to Babaji.

I'm surprised you said to Babaji. I thought you were going to say to you or to God. Why did you say to Babaji?

Babaji is your teacher now Connie. Go toward Babaji. Babaji is your narrow channel to me and God.

I thought that if one just called or asked for Babaji, he would always come, be with them and help them reach you?

He will be there, yes. But you will need to release all separation to unite with him fully and with me.

Jesus, why am I feeling so pulled to Babaji and you even more now?

We are opening your heart to me. God follows me. When you unite with me, you find God.

When you say, unite with me, do you mean reach or obtain your depth and level of love, compassion and non-judgment?

Yes, Connie. Yes.

And again Jesus, what is your definition of God?

Your creator; my creator; all energy in the universe; total fullness.

Jan 20, 2011

Babaji, today I saw a Youtube video of Eckart Tolle. He talked about how some say the only way to reach enlightenment is to be fully in the present—not to try to reach anything. That the very act of trying to get somewhere else that's in the future is not being fully in the present, not fully accepting the present moment as it is; that this keeps one in ego, not God consciousness; enlightenment.

He referred to other people saying, as you just recently did also, that one needs to yearn, pine for, call God deeply, beg for God, implying this is needed to reach God. I have heard this before also and have been confused by these two differing ideologies. What Eckhart Tolle said was so enlightening! But then I felt disheartened because I cannot really understand how this is possible to accomplish. How can one be completely accepting in the present moment as it is, without having God awareness, but desire, call, yearn for God at the same time?

You cannot do both at the same time. You experience one and then the other. Each time you are deeper in one of these times, you are closer to the other.

How is that?

When you yearn deeply for God, more peace comes with the present.

That doesn't make total sense to me.

It will. Yearn for God and he will bring you more peace. Connie, share our conversations with everyone.

I feel like I've been yearning for God my entire adult life and I'm not near being in peace!

You have not been yearning like you are now Connie, now that I am with you.

Well, that is certainly true.

Yes . . . be a servant of God by helping to teach others how to be with God. There is no greater gift.

Babaji. Are you going to be reborn as a human on this planet again?

Yes. I already am.

Really? Where are you? Who are you?

I am not known to anyone as anyone.

Are you going to be?

Yes.

Is your own spirit in a human form on this planet right now?

Yes, Connie, it is true.

Can I ask where you are?

In my homeland. I always return my homeland.

Why not anywhere else?

It is my favorite place.

Why is it your favorite place? Is it the energy of the collective consciousness there, the memories you had there, the terrain or climate?

It is because it is where I was initially born.

Are you going to be another spiritual teacher to people in the world?

Yes, Connie, I am.

Can I ask when?

Yes. Not now.

That's all you're going to say about that?

Yes. Not now. I am coming back though again for everyone.

I am presuming most or all of us have re-incarnated many lifetimes. I have heard that you have several times as a spiritual teacher to the people in the world to spread knowledge and understanding of how to obtain awareness of our true selves; enlightenment; God. Is this true?

Yes, I have.

You must care about us a lot to continue doing this? Is there any other reason?

No. That is the only reason.

This might be a dumb question, but if I were enlightened, as you are, I think I might just prefer to bask in experiencing and being God's love. I'm not sure I would want to do anything else but continue to enjoy experiencing that without any worldy distractions. You don't ever feel this way?

No, Connie. My love continues to expand more and more as I help enlighten one by one.

Really? How is that?

Connie, the love you feel when you bring enlightenment to only one person is enough to bring you to God's feet for all eternity. It is not able to be described, only experienced. I weep with such honor to our Father when I help someone achieve enlightenment. I become one all over again.

Wow. That's a very interesting answer. That is a most beautiful answer.

It is, yes.

I'm a little speechless again right now.

It is beautiful to start feeling more love, isn't it?

Yes, Babaji. It is. Do you have anything else you'd like to say right now?

Yes, I do. I want everyone to tell everyone they know they appreciate having them in their life and to think of why.

Ok. Why do you say that?

Everyone in your life, in everyone's life, is there to help give you the experiences you need to become more aware of your true selves, to heighten your level of awareness, to help you learn how to love yourself and others more fully. That's why all of you are here; to experience life in this physical world with the full awareness of who you really are; who you are beyond the physical. Everyone is a catalyst for each other—especially the people that cause you pain.

If someone caused or is causing you any pain, it is because you needed or are needing that experience to be capable of continuing to evolve spiritually. Whether you presently understand this or not, know they are to be appreciated and honored for what they are giving you that you need. Count your blessings. Everyone in your life is a blessing.

Why do personal relationships often seem to be the most challenging for many?

Because the closest people in your life, mirror to you your very deepest fears.

Can you explain more about that? How?

Yes. The closer someone is to you, the closer you reach the deepest issues in your heart.

And you define the deepest issues in your heart as . . . ?

Self-hatred.

That sounds kind of terrible.

It is only terrible when you are self-loathing.

What do you mean by that?

It is terrible to have self-loathing, yes.

Why do we have self-loathing?

Because you have such deep guilt for leaving God.

How did we leave God? I know I never would have done that on purpose!

No one does it on purpose.

Then why do we?

Because you allowed the ego to make you ignorant.

Ignorant of what?

Ignorant of knowing yourself as being God.

Why would anyone do that?

Because you felt fear from leaving God.

How/why/could/would we do that?

Because you allowed the ego to make you ignorant.

Can't we experience life in the physical world without allowing the ego to make us ignorant?

Yes. But it is rare.

Why?

Because when you are born, you have a split second to make a choice. One usually feels the pain of birth and if you are not able to release that pain, you accept the ego into your mind.

Do you mind explaining that more?

When one is born, they are in a limited, restricted physical body and that alone creates division. Very few are able to accept it immediately without judging it.

How does one judge it?

As fear.

Is this what the Bible refers to as the original sin? As soon as we're born, we have, what the bible refers to as automatically have "sinned"— meaning, we have "turned our backs on God" because we lost the awareness that we are God, unlimited and omnipresent starting at the moment of birth?

Yes, Connie. Yes.

It seems quite unfair to have to start out life in this way—in such a state of ignorance of God.

It was your choice to be born in a physical body.

Why on earth would one choose that if it meant leaving God, God awareness?

To have fun and play in your make believe world.

I think I'm going to have to absorb and contemplate that before I can ask anything more about this.

Yes, Connie. Absorb my words and feel my love for Christ and you while you are absorbing.

Do you mind me asking you all these questions?

No. You and I are teachers of knowledge together now.

Jan 21, 2011

Babaji, I'm grateful that I learned of who you are and that I am able to communicate to you and that you care enough about me to be giving me your time like this. I truly felt more peace upon waking this morning, which was shocking! I normally wake up feeling such an uncomfortable anxiety, dreading another long, stressful day ahead. My nervous system felt more relaxed for the first time in a long time.

I actually felt a mild, but noticeable deeper level of inner peace. Did you help do this? Is this because I've been regularly listening to this Youtube video that repeats your mantra in a song, intentionally feeling a particular emotional pain as fully as I can?

Oh, yes. Face, feel and accept your pain; your suppressed, repressed past emotional pains. When you do, they literally leave your body and developing more inner peace is inevitable.

Thank you from the bottom of my heart.

You are more than welcome. I want to tell you more about our personal journey together to Christ. I am going to burn your ego away with fire. It will be a very quick death.

Seriously?

Yes, seriously.

That's sounds a little freaky—scary! What on earth does that mean?

It will signify the birth of Christ in you.

But Jesus died on the cross.

He began a new beginning on it. He died and transformed into a new existence after those few moments of pain, separation and fear he spoke of to you before, when he described to you what he experienced on the cross. He overcame it quickly after he gave into it, like he said. He created a conquering of all egos on this planet by 2052. It will be done.

All the people on this planet are going to be enlightened by then?! That sounds hard to believe.

Yes. That's when he chose this to happen.

He died on the cross a long time ago. Why did he wait so long for this to happen?

He knew the exact time it would take for this. Now, about our journey to Christ together. I will take care of everything for you if you continue listening to my mantra as you have been, talk to me every day and share my words to the world.

Ok. I will. But, what does that accomplish?

You are teaching others how to reach God by sharing our conversations. You must give this willingly and with gratitude— just long enough to receive God's grace. If you want Christ consciousness, you need to help others acquire it. You need to be giving what you want to receive.

Does that apply to everyone or just me?

Everyone. You are going to pour your heart out much more to me and Christ next week. It will not be scary for a moment. We need to delve into some of your pain now. We will do this together. I will direct you.

Personal note: Babaji asked me a few questions (given later) that got me honed in on a particular pain from my past. It was regarding the pain I felt when I was three years old and thereafter from my father choosing to leave my life. I was actually very surprised this deep pain came out since I thought I already fully healed from this.

For several minutes I was crying and just allowed myself to feel the specific pain of how I felt about my father abandoning me and my brother. I felt deep feelings of being unloved, not cared about, that I must be defective in some way because my father did not love or care about me enough to choose to stay in my life. I've actually always wished my father had been a drunk or drug addict, was unemployed and struggling with life so much, he was extremely challenged handling being a father to me and my brother or that he had a horrible, abusive childhood. It would be much easier for me to understand why he left me and I would not have taken it so personally. I remained close with his parents my whole life, who were the most idyllic parents and grandparents. He was raised in a stable, upper middle class family and had the most loving and devoted parents. My father had his own business and was successful from the age of 18. It's been so much more painful for me to know that there wasn't any other reason other than he simply did not love or care about me enough.

I felt the fearfulness and insecurity I've always felt since I can remember as a young child because I didn't have my father in my life. I was blessed to have such a loving, devoted mother. But understandably, she was always bogged down, struggling to keep a roof over our heads and food on the table. I never felt secure or safe or that everything was going to be ok. I intentionally felt these feelings deeply and intensely. I have to say, it was not enjoyable. After several minutes, the feelings just quickly faded away.

That was perfect Connie.

I know Jesus is with me always. But, even though I can communicate to Jesus also, I actually feel you are really with me; more than I can with Jesus. Why?

Yes. A devotee of Christ can sometimes reach you deeper because we are more solid in your mind. Continue talking with me.

All I want to do is be alone, listen to your mantra and talk to you and write down our conversations.

Yes, I am pulling your heart to me.

Why?

You need to yearn now Connie. That is all you need to do now; listen to my mantra and share my words to the world.

Why do I need to yearn?

Connie, yearn for me so deeply—for Jesus—for God.

But, again, why is that important?

Connie, yearning for us heals and opens your heart. It's destroying the ego so quickly now. When you yearn for us, God always comes.

I just recently read on your website (babaji.net) the actual meaning of your mantra. It means "I surrender to you God" or "Lord, thy will be done". But, what's the value in saying or hearing it? I feel I've been intentionally surrendering myself to God since I was 21 years old!

Saying, hearing or thinking it is calls God deeper, harder more intensely than anything you could ever do—literally.

Really? That seems weird. Why? How?

It is a sound that God cannot resist.

But, why? How?

Sound effects for humans on this planet create an energy in your body that changes your DNA. Some sounds affect it positively, some negatively. It is the make-up of the human body.

Now, I'm totally confused.

The rays of light from the sun is energy that strongly effects the human body. Sounds do too, down to your DNA. Your DNA changes when you are enlightened. The sound of this mantra, even when said silently in your mind automatically changes your DNA to that of an enlightened person's DNA.

That's sounds unbelievable.

Connie, everything in this universe affects your DNA.

How many times do you feel is ideal to say, hear or think your mantra? Daily? Weekly?

At least 109 times daily.

Why exactly at least 109 times?

108 times is enough to open every energy channel in the human body. The extra one is for uniting them all as one.

How very interesting and intriguing. What exactly is an energy channel?

They are invisible locations in the body. If they are closed from emotional pain, this disenables them to be perfectly balanced.

This energy in your body needs to be perfectly balanced to be enlightened.

Well, that is totally baffling! Is emotional pain the only thing that imbalances these energy channels in the body?

Yes.

Don't physical toxins in the body imbalance these energy channels?

No. Not these.

That's hard to imagine. Does a physical health condition imbalance them?

No.

If these energy channels are in the physical body, how can the condition of the physical body not affect them?

They are not affected by anything in the physical world, only your emotions.

I know meditation releases stress energy. What else does?

Sleeping, dreaming and loving are a few.

Wow, I'm mystified. But apparently, saying your mantra also does?

No. Repetition of my mantra does not directly release stress energy from these energy channels. Repetition of my mantra balances them without releasing stress first. Saying, hearing or thinking it puts the cart before the horse. Instead of releasing stress to balance these channels, repetition of my mantra directly balances these channels and then forces the emotional stress out.

Double wow! That's why I've been having all of these bizarre, involuntary intense emotional releases in the last week, since I started listening to your video so many times every day!? The same thing has been happening to my other two friends also since they started listening to your video every day! So, only sounds directly balance these energy channels?

Only one sound; my mantra.

That is baffling. Why do we have these energy channels? What are they there for?

They are a form of a defense mechanism. You could not live without them. They absorb emotional stress—like a shock absorber.

Does emotional stress accumulate in these energy channels over time?

Yes.

Are they able to release and rid of the emotional stress in some way?

Yes. Anything that releases emotional stress, removes the emotional stress from these channels. When all of these energy channels are free from negative energy, which is unhealed pain from your past experiences, they are perfectly balanced. Enlightenment is then inevitable.

How interesting!

Yes, Connie.

You've got me speechless again.

The more you listen to or repeat this mantra, the more emotional stress energy that has been suppressed and repressed will be forced out through balancing these energy channels.

Jan 22, 2011

I started talking to Babaji about a particular personal issue in my life that I was worried about. He responded with the following statement.

Connie, I conquer ego.

But, Jesus does too, right? I'm just curious. I feel grateful to have you in my life as my father, my spiritual teacher, but, why wouldn't God just have Jesus take care of what we need?

It takes the two of us Connie.

Is that just for me, certain people or everyone?

Everyone.

That doesn't make sense. Why is that?

Jesus heals one's heart with love, compassion and non-judgment and when you are ready, I come in and take over. There is no one that does not go through me to reach our beloved Christ.

When you say that, do you mean that one needs to fully conquer their ego? I would think some or many have and can eventually do that without your direct help, either on their own or with the help of another spiritual teacher or Devotee of Christ?

They may get close, but they need me to finish the task. Often times, people do not know of me until they are near ready.

What about people that are religious and will never be open to asking for a spiritual teacher not of their own religion or background? What happens to them then?

Connie, eventually they will.

That really surprises me to hear that. No other enlightened spiritual teachers or saints can get one to full enlightenment?

No, Connie. I will explain why. There are two beings that get one to God fully and they are Jesus and I both together—Jesus heals the heart and I conquer the ego.

That makes sense in one way, but doesn't in another way.

There's no other way Connie. Eventually, one will be lead you to Christ and then to me. When I have helped one overcome their ego, I hand them back to Christ and he takes them to God.

Well, that's very interesting. You know I myself, could care less who it is! But some people will want it to be someone of their own religion or culture. So, I think there may be some people that are not going to want to hear that or believe it.

I know Connie.

Well, how come I never heard of this before or you until just recently?

Because you were not ready for me Connie until recently.

You'd think the Bible would have talked about you then? Why not?

Because the people were not ready for me then.

That sounds kind of odd to me.

Connie, it's ok.

Well, good, I'm glad to hear that! Thank you, Babaji.

I will never NOT be there for someone that is ready for me. When they are, they will hear of me and when they call my name, I will be there.

I read on your website that you urged the people to follow the religion that is in their heart. You said that every religion leads to the same divine goal and that you had come to revive the eternal and ageless religion, the Sanatan Dharma; the three basic principles: Truth, Simplicity, and Love. You emphasized constant repetition of the ancient Sanskrit mantra Om Namah Shivaya and to live in harmony along with selfless service to humanity.

Yes, Connie. That is true. There will be one universal religion in time. A religion that accepts all religions with love and honor— that is my religion.

Well, Babaji. That sounds like a dream come true! I'm sure that will require some major miracles! So many people negatively judge and even hate and kill people just for having a different religion than their own, all in the name of God. It's insanity!

Yes, Connie. That is why mass destruction is coming to Earth. It is time to grow, like it or not.

Do you want to say anything else specific or do you want me to ask you something?

Tell me what's on your mind.

I feel a little, or I should say more than a little sad. I just feel sad, just plain lonely, kind of numb a little.

Why?

I'm bored with my life. I'm not living a life that I want or enjoy. I feel that I am missing so much, what could be enjoyable, treasured times in life. There are a lot of other reasons too. Not to mention, I've been living in pretty much total isolation 98% of the time for one a half years since I moved here to Daytona. I'm sure you'll even agree, this empty, poverty stricken town does not have a positive, enhancing energy. It's pretty depressing just living here period. But my life is truly joyless. Except for the fulfillment I get from being able to help my clients, I have literally no joy, no fun, no laughter. It's just stress and frustration. I'm always worried about having to handle all of these financial responsibilities and also about some uncertainties I have in my personal life.

Needless to say, also the ten years of being totally bed-ridden when I was mercury poisoned and my back injury completely debilitated me. On top of that ten year experience, I've now spent the last year and a half like this—in more total isolation?! I'm 43 years old. I have only wanted one thing in my life, other than good health and enlightenment—to be a wife and mother and financially secure; to have a nice, simple family life. I acquired financial security at a rather young age, but lost it all because of having severe health issues with enormous medical expenses for ten years!

And I don't have a husband or a family yet. I never could have imagined being where I am in my life right now. I feel like I have gone backwards in life in all areas. I used to meditate 2 hours twice a day, faithfully for years. Now, I can't even discipline myself enough to meditate 20 minutes twice a day. Even though I can talk to you, Jesus or any of my angels anytime, which I am more than grateful for, I don't feel in tune with or connected with God as I did before. My life is just too stressful. I work so much with two jobs now, I barely have time to eat a meal.

It is good to know why you are depressed, Connie.

Ok, Babaji.

Now, Connie, for another lesson from me. I want you to allow yourself to be depressed. Feel it intently now. You are alone now.

I'm not really in the mood to right now, but, of course, I will . . . ok.

Personal note:

After ten minutes of lying down thinking of all the things that's making me feel sad and disappointed with life, I checked in with Babaji. He said, "you're doing well Connie, keep going". The whole time, I'm calmly, silently telling Babaji all the reasons and then 5-10 minutes later, I told him that it's just torture living here in this physical world so limited and helpless to create a happy life, a life really worth living.

Then I started crying and felt that sadness and disappointment with some frustration also for 2-3 minutes. Then I was back to my normal calm state.

Was that enough? Good for now Babaji?

Yes. Very good.

Is there anything in particular you want to talk about? I don't really have anything in particular to ask. I'm just kind of blah tonight.

Listen to my mantra a little longer and then go to sleep.

Sunday, Jan 22, 2011

I was thinking about what you said earlier about mass destruction coming to this planet. Are there going to be a lot of problems coming to the people on this planet?

Yes, Connie. There's going to be a storm and it's going to destroy everyone on this planet that is not ready.

I'm assuming you mean people that are not ready to love enough or reach a higher level of consciousness? Do you mean a real storm or are you saying that word symbolically, meaning something is going to create massive destruction on this planet?

Symbolically. There will be massive destruction on this planet, yes.

Well, a lot of cultures and civilizations have been predicting something like this happening around 2012 or thereafter. What kind(s) of destruction? Do you really want me to share these conversations with other people?

Yes, the world needs to hear this.

Ok. But, I'm not fully comfortable with that. I'm not sure if I feel comfortable openly talking about negative things like this.

A human made catastrophe.

Can you say exactly what?

Yes. A war situation.

That sounds like maybe a World War Three?

Yes. It will be the last war on Earth.

You don't want me to share this information with others, do you!?

Do not leave out a word. You are learning how to overcome the last fears your ego has hold on you. No more hiding anything of your true self Connie. You cannot escape them any longer now that I am with you. Jesus has healed your heart, yes—enough to be ready to conquer your ego, when you are ready for this, God brings Babaji.

I'm taken aback, yet again Babaji.

Yes. Next time, let's talk more about your healing gift coming— not what you do now as an Intuitive Communicator or Holistic Health Practitioner, but your purpose as a direct healer. If you are afraid to be your true self to the world, you will not reach your full purpose—as a direct healer. Remember this Connie.

I don't get the healing part, but ok.

Jan 23, 2011

Babaji, last night I couldn't think of much to say or ask about. Now, I have so many different things to ask you, I don't know where to begin.

Yes, Connie. It is time to share more with the world.

I just don't know where to begin; what to ask right now.

Yes, your mind is full now?

Yes, it is.

Listen to my mantra a little more first.

Ok. I'm very nervous about my interview for an additional part-time job/career opportunity today—uncomfortably nervous.

Your ego loves you nervous, doesn't it?

Yes, I guess you're right.

Connie, why do you feel so nervous?

It's ridiculous that I do, I know. I consider myself very good at what I do and certainly well experienced. I guess I'm afraid they're going to feel I'm not good enough. Or maybe it's because I'm so attached to the outcome. I am really desperate for this job because I need the money so badly. It's been such a struggle getting me and my two businesses more seen and heard having no money to invest in marketing or advertising.

Yes, Connie.

Personal note: I started crying and said to Babaji . . . "I don't feel good enough". I was feeling so deeply how I didn't feel good enough—not at what I did for a living, but simply as a person, with anything and everything. For about ten minutes, I continued crying and deeply felt how I felt not good enough.

Connie, you did well feeling the pain that was there.

Thank you, Babaji.

Several minutes later . . .

I suddenly remembered how I felt when I was going to kindergarten the first day and didn't want to leave my mom. This memory just popped into my mind out of nowhere! I was fearful and franticly desperate to stay with my mom so badly that day. I just sat there crying, feeling exactly how I felt at that moment my first day of kindergarten when my mom was about to leave me. I didn't really understand why I was feeling this. After all, it was just an experience I went through as a young child. I felt a little embarrassed feeling this way so strongly, but as an adult. But, I just went with it and allowed myself to feel that feeling—the fear, the panic, the fear of being abandoned. I stayed with it for several minutes and then it just simply went away. After that experience, I went to my job interview.

Babaji, the interview went great. I don't know why I was so nervous.

Yes, Connie. The ego is so powerful when you believe in it.

You sure are right about that. How can I not believe in it Babaji? I just don't know how not to.

You allow it to be and laugh at it.

Jan 24, 2011

Babaji, I don't really feel comfortable sharing parts of these conversations we've had where we are talking about some personal experiences of mine. I don't mind revealing my vulnerabilities, but some of this stuff is personal! Aren't I entitled to a little privacy with complete strangers for goodness sakes?

Connie, please share it with everyone. Please share revealing your true self to everyone in the world so you can help them grow to God.

Alright, Babaji. I guess I'll think about it.

You will gain more than you know in doing so.

Well, now that you said that, it's probably going to be hard for me not to.

Yes, Connie. Feel your heart and never be afraid to reveal your true self. You create so much separation with God when you do.

All I seem to want to do is be alone, listen to your mantra and talk to you.

Yes, Connie. That is my love for you—drawing you to me.

I'm really blown away by all the things that have been happening spontaneously to me since I started talking to you and listening to your mantra. I've been having a lot of involuntary emotional releases. Sometimes I'm fine and normal, then the next moment I feel deep pain, fear, sorrow or regret about something particular or for no identifiable reason and then I'm fine and normal again. Then I start to spontaneously feel such a deep yearning to be closer to you, to Jesus, to God. I feel so alone and separate from Jesus and God more than ever. Not to sound overly dramatic, but it is tormenting. Every spare minute I have, I want to listen to your mantra and talk to you. It is baffling.

It is not baffling. It is because you feel my love pulling you to me, to Christ, to God. Connie, I want to talk more about your purpose now. You need to get something well understood. You are not going to continue to be an Intuitive Communicator or Holistic Health Practitioner for the rest of your life. You are a healer now, but you are destined to be healing people in a different way. You are so close now Connie to allowing God in.

When you become one with me and Christ, your new journey begins. There's one thing you must remember—always be honest.

Ok. Why do you say that?

If you are ever dishonest, you will fall out of your path.

That's it?

Yes.

Gosh, I hope I don't accidentally screw up.

If you are honest, you will remain in Christ consciousness and a healer.

What about when I say to a client during a phone consultation I'm going to get a beverage and I'm really going to the restroom? What about an innocent, little white lie like that?

Never, ever be dishonest.

I hope I don't slip and screw up sometime!

This conversation will prevent that Connie.

You surprised me with that comment Babaji.

Jan 25, 2011

Babaji, I feel so bad that I'm still smoking, as I'm sure you know. I've been smoking a few months now and I still haven't quit.

Allow yourself to quit by allowing yourself to accept it.

Babaji, I wish I didn't have to wake up and go through each day. I wish I could just be where you are. I don't want to live anymore. I don't want to live this life anymore. I'm not suicidal, as I'm sure you know. But, I feel so trapped and stuck in this world living such an unhealthy, over-worked, stressful life and still never having enough money for the bare basics of my needs.

I've had no top molar teeth for over a year now since my two bridges and crown broke, all in the same month! It's so painful every time I eat without having teeth. It tears up my gums. I've had a small spot on my chest for over a year that my doctor said is skin cancer that I can't *afford to get surgically removed. I desperately need an eye exam and glasses. It's not easy going around all day with blurry vision! I can't afford my dog's monthly heartworm and flea medicine anymore. That alone is $50 a month. I dread waking up every day to my life. There is no joy in it when just struggling to survive like this. It's not a life worth living in my opinion and probably in anyone's opinion.*

Connie, I know what it's like. I've been there before. Connie, feel the pain of being stuck where you are. Yes, feel it intently.

I'm tired of handling life with all these responsibilities. I just paid nearly $800 for new tires I had to get for my car. That has set me back again so much. Last month it was an expensive car repair bill. You said before we chose to be in a physical body to have fun and play in our make believe world. Well, I'm not able to have fun and play. I'm not able to experience what I consider a fun and enjoyable life.

Yes. I know. Your ego does not want you to have fun and play. Until you conquer your ego, you will have short-lived experiences that you enjoy, if you are one of the fortunate ones. And even then, it is child's play—a very limited experience of enjoying life. When you have God in your awareness, then and only then will you understand the meaning of fun. And I will get you there as my teacher did me.

Thank you, Babaji.

Now start your day and be as happy as you can.

Ok, Babaji.

Let the wheel of maya (the illusion of what we think is reality in the physical world) continue and you will reach the beginning of reality—true reality.

Babaji, I'm having a little difficulty getting in touch with the pain that's in my heart. Any suggestions?

If you cannot identify a pain in your heart right now, think back to an earlier time in your life, a particular memory; an experience that caused you to feel pain in some way. Identify that specific pain, that specific feeling. Then try to remember another experience when you were younger, when you felt that same type of pain and then again, until you remember your earliest experience that made you feel the same way. That is what you want to feel—the pain from that experience. You need to give it your undistracted attention, fully.

This is what heals the pain in the heart and conquers ego. All the judgments that have been created by your ego's perception of your experiences dissolves away as your past pains are healed and released. Remember not to think of the person or circumstance that made you feel bad, simply be willing to feel the pain you felt then. You will continue to create experiences that mimic that pain until it has been acknowledged and felt fully; until it has been honored. When it is honored, you will not continue to unconsciously create experiences that manifest the same form of pain.

How very interesting! I get it. Is that why many people, including myself seem to go through life making the same mistakes over and over, creating a similar unwanted outcome again and again, just with someone new or in a different way? So, this pattern will continue until that person heals that particular pain in their heart?

Yes, that is right Connie.

Thanks Babaji!

I wonder how long it's going to take to heal all the pain in my heart Babaji. Do you know?

It depends on many things Connie. The most important thing you can do to heal the heart is to do 'my work'. Do it as often as you can. It's very effective.

What other things does it depend on?

Mainly, on how willing you are to face and feel your pain.

Jan 27, 2011

Babaji, I've wondered for many years about what happened to an enlightened spiritual teacher that was my spiritual guru for a long time. He changed in the latter years of his life in a way I do not consider was good. Is it appropriate to ask you about this? Do you know?

Yes.

Should I write this down so I share it with everyone or just keep this to myself?

Share it with everyone Connie; everything. Some wonder the exact same thing. It will bring more peace, understanding and compassion.

Ok.

He went backwards on the wheel of maya, Connie.

Was he really enlightened? If so, I don't understand how one that is, can then go backwards.

He was not, no. But, he was close. Then guess what happened, Connie? When his devotee of Christ died, his spiritual teacher, he lost his devotion along with him. His ego replaced it. That is a tricky time when one is so close. Without studious devotion, the ego creeps in behind your back. Clever, the ego is. A devotee of Christ is needed more than ever then.

But, I'm presuming he stayed devoted to his spiritual teacher, even after he died?

Yes, but his ego took over without his spiritual teacher's supervision.

But, I'm sure his spiritual teacher was still with him, supervising him, even though he wasn't in a physical body anymore, wasn't he?

Yes, but without his spiritual teacher in the physical world anymore, he turned to himself then—his ego—his ego's pain.

That sounds a little sad. Why didn't Jesus or God send him another spiritual teacher so that wouldn't happen?

He was not open to another. He left his spiritual path after his spiritual teacher left his body and he went backwards.

This man was my spiritual teacher for many years. I personally witnessed his greed, his selfishness, his lack of compassion for others, his lack of integrity and even blatant dishonesty. How could he suddenly become all that; so different than how he was before, when he was so close to enlightenment at one time? That is confusing to me. It was so disheartening for me to witness this.

His ego snuck in again. He was attached to one thing then in the physical world—his spiritual teacher. When his teacher died, he allowed the judgment of that separation to supersede his level of love and devotion to God.

Life sounds terrible Babaji.

When you are attached to the ego, it is.

But, he just had so much love for his spiritual teacher; love! That was a good thing, right?

Love, yes; attachment to anything or anyone in this physical world, no.

It's impossible to love someone deeply and not be attached to them Babaji. If you wouldn't care if they died, you wouldn't love them very much.

Loving through the ego always brings attachment to what you love. Love from who you really are; that level of loving is miniscule in comparison. When you love from having the awareness that you ARE love itself, there is no such thing as separation.

I have one client in particular, that consults with me to communicate to her deceased husband. Her spouse died over a few years ago and she is still in so much pain from her loss. She is often either angry or sad and filled with grief. If I had such a wonderful loving partnership with someone for so many years as she clearly did, I don't think I'd ever be able to get over it and be happy without him again either. It just sounds so horrible Babaji.

Connie, it is the ultimate of horrible when you lose a beloved. The only way you can resolve this issue is to become enlightened. You need three things to become enlightened; all love, all compassion and all non-judgment. The only thing keeping you from experiencing all love, all compassion and all non-judgment is the pain in your heart, created by your ego's perception; your judgments; your fears. The only way to heal your pain is to face it and feel it fully—until it is gone.

Well, thanks for answering these questions about my previous spiritual teacher. I've been confused about this for a long time.

Never, ever lose your devotion to me or Christ.

I don't think I could if I tried.

No, you will not.

But again Babaji, why is having devotion so important?

Your devotion to the right spiritual teacher withers away the ego, Connie.

How?

The devotion you are feeling is love Connie. When you have a spiritual teacher that is all loving, all compassionate and all non-judgmental, that teacher is capable of teaching you what you need, as you need it. Enlightenment is a state of awareness achieved when you have surrendered the ego. An enlightened teacher teaches one how to do that.

If his spiritual teacher didn't die when he did, would he have reached full enlightenment with his teacher's assistance alone? Or would he eventually have had to replace his devotion for his teacher to you? [regarding what you said earlier]

Not replace it away from his teacher to me, but transfer it to me.

I still find that so strange that there is no one other than you that is capable of fully assisting one to Christ consciousness. There are other enlightened Devotees of Christ and spiritual teachers that have the desire and purpose to help bring enlightenment to people too, aren't there?

Yes. But, no one can take them to our beloved Christ but me. I am not a person, place or thing Connie. I am the creation of an energy that has the qualities that are needed to conquer ego. Jesus is an energy that has the qualities needed to heal the heart. Christ and I are the full path to God realization.

But, Jesus was a human on this planet. You were too and still are as you said.

Yes, Christ was also in human form before and I am still on earth in human form. But, we created the qualities needed to reach God awareness.

Ok. I think I'm starting to get it now! I've already learned that Jesus's qualities are all love, all compassion and all non-judgment. What exactly are your qualities?

I am the non-judgment Connie. They are together as one. You must surrender the ego to be free of all judgment. You need to feel enough love and compassion to have non-judgment. The pain in your heart is what prevents you from experiencing the love that you already are. The only way to heal the pain in your heart is to face it and feel it fully; honor it. The pain in your heart is a result of how your ego perceives all your experiences and your ego always perceives everything without love, as separate from love—as fear.

All the pains in your heart are various forms of your fear. Your ego needs to feel justified for feeling them, otherwise it could not exist. Fear is the path of survival for the ego. The ego is your fear. It needs to continue existing and it does this through feeling more forms of fear (anger, resentment, sorrow, grief, inadequacy, dissatisfaction, incompleteness, loneliness, worry). So, it will continue to find various reasons throughout life to feel justified for having these different negative emotions. Remember this Connie. Whenever you need to feel justified for feeling any pain, know you already are justified for feeling that way. You have all the good reasons on earth to be justified. Then just feel the pain that is there—until it is gone.

So, to reiterate . . . Jesus basically heals one's heart; the pain in their heart with love and compassion, which in turn, creates non-judgment. You help one surrender their ego by facing and feeling their pain, which is created by the ego's perception of all experiences, which is totally fear-based, right?

Yes, Connie, yes. The heart is Jesus's specialty, the ego is mine.

How interesting! I am really getting it now. I was thinking about how Jesus seems to have a personality, an energy about him that is so loving, allowing, compassionate, soft, gentle, patient and kind of passive. You seem to have an energy that is also loving, allowing and compassionate too, but a more pro-active, conquering, warrior-type of energy, more directly spoken in your speech also. Do you agree?

Yes, Connie. Healing the heart requires different qualities than conquering the ego.

Yes, I think I understand now. It takes love and compassion to heal the heart and it takes strength and courage to face and feel the ego's pains and judgments, right?

Yes. Let's listen to my mantra now.

Ok.

Personal note: I intentionally felt the deep sorrow, loss and frustration I had about losing my once "ideal" life, before when I was financially secure and had my needs met, had a nice, comfortable home, a balanced life and was able to do things I enjoyed. Just simple things like going to the beach, going to dinner with a friend, dating, working out at the gym or going to a yoga class, a little shopping here and there. I ate incredibly well and enjoyed being able to eat well and take good care of my body. I certainly didn't smoke then. I meditated every day. I didn't have much stress in my life and certainly no major financial worries every day. I felt the deep pain from missing my once nice life to where I am stuck now.

Later . . .

Babaji, I'm listening to the song that plays your mantra again. Anything you'd like me to do now? I hope you're not going to suggest I feel some more pain?

No. What questions do you have?

My friend that I spoke to today for the first time in a long time is a strict catholic. She talked about how the Bible says Jesus literally gets jealous if someone loves another, especially if a partner is loved as much as or more than Him. Of course I didn't even think of mentioning that I communicate directly to Jesus! I know that would not have gone over *very well. I felt sad for her not understanding that one does not have to limit their level of love for someone! It's not as if she has only ten pounds of love available and if she gives some of it to someone else, it's taking some away from Jesus. I wanted so much to tell her that when she loves someone else, she is also loving Jesus; that Jesus **is** her love; that Jesus is trying to teach us how to love others and ourselves more! I've noticed that many religious people tend to have so much guilt, fear and shame instilled in them from their religion. What do you think about that?*

Connie, everyone has guilt, fear and shame until they are with Christ (Christ consciousness).

Yes, I understand. Can you start a topic please? I am drawing a blank.

Be silent everyday please. Have time for silence every day.

I don't even have to ask the benefits of that—I already know. It's been an unsuccessful challenge for me to do this daily. It's uncomfortable for me to sit there in silence. I feel how much anxiety and stress I have in my nervous system and whole body even more. And I am not in a position financially to improve the quality of my life. I'm simply not. It is so disheartening.

Yes. That is the purpose of meditating, Connie. It stills, relaxes and pacifies the nervous system and mind. When you silence the mind, the ego becomes passive.

Yes, I know.

Start tomorrow Connie, please.

Ok Babaji. I'll try.

A spiritual teacher needs not from you.

What does that mean?

Needs nothing.

Please explain?

Sees what you need and tells you.

Personal note: As soon as I woke up, still in bed, I instantly felt fearful as my mind was now conscious again and awake. I was intensely fearful that I was still in my body. I was horrified knowing I was going to be trapped in my body the whole day ahead of me. I felt such a deep feeling of dread. My mind instantly started racing with fear and panic and then for the first time in my life, I felt true self-hatred and self-loathing. It is indescribable. I so deeply hated who I was, who I had become. Nearly two years ago, when I still lived in Jupiter, I was in great physical shape since I worked out nearly every day, ate an impeccably healthy diet, didn't smoke, I didn't drink cocktails, wine or coffee.

I was thinking how I hadn't worked out in over a year now, how nutritionally depleted and exhausted I was, how stressful my life was with such financial worries. I didn't have my mom to visit, no friends, I lived in a moldy, disgusting apartment in a really bad neighborhood. There was absolutely nothing to do in this town except going to a riff-raff bar. I didn't have the time, energy or money to do anything anyway. Coping with such financial worries day after day was so grueling and defeating. I had such a lack of motivation and joy for life and continued getting more and more depressed. I thought about how I didn't walk my dogs in the park everyday anymore, usually only 1-2 times a week and what a chore is was to me now, not a pleasure like it used to be.

I started drinking wine sometimes to help numb the depression, stress and worry. I eventually broke down and started smoking. I thought about how I had been taking sleeping pills for the first time in my life for over six months just so I could sleep. I felt like garbage every day. I barely laughed or smiled anymore. When I did, it was a fake smile.

I was noticing the extreme contrast of how I was now compared to how I used to be; a vital, happy, cheerful pillar of health not long ago. These last couple years, I have become everything I despised the most—an unhealthy, undisciplined, poverty-stricken, miserable low-life. Nearly every month I was getting some utility cut off because I couldn't pay it. Last time at the gas station, I paid eight quarters for gas in my car. I never felt so low about myself . . .

I have a question Babaji. Is it true that what we believe creates and becomes our reality? And that our beliefs are created by our ego's perception; from how our ego perceived all of our past experiences?

Yes, Connie. Go back and read Jesus's words from a conversation you had with him before.

Yes, I remember some of what he said. I will read it again. But, my inner beliefs must really be messed up Babaji!

Yes, they are. Everyone's beliefs are damaging until they know they are God. Until then, everyone will create suffering in their lives in one form to the next. Connie, you are a teacher now.

I am NOT the teacher—you and Jesus are. Unfortunately, I am most definitely a student in learning.

Anyone sharing our knowledge is a teacher. Since you have agreed to share this, to be your true self, to stop feeling shameful for the special gift you have, being Jesus's sibling, God's child, a devotee of Christ, every beautiful and unique aspect of who you are—you will awaken; awaken to our beloved Christ.

Jan 31, 2011

Let's start with another lesson.

Ok.

Have you intentionally felt the pain you've had the last few days?

Ah . . . I don't think so, no.

Now is a good time. You are alone.

Ok. But, I have a feeling of dread about this.

I know Connie. It's time to face it.

Ok.

What have you been feeling most the last few days?

Shame and guilt that I'm still smoking. Feeling horrible physically. Feeling pretty low in every sense of the word.

Yes, now tell me why?

Because I lost everything due to severe health issues with enormous medical expenses and live a majorly stressful and struggling life! I could get into more detail, but need I say more?! Look how my life is every day. I can barely afford to pay rent every month and feed myself and my dogs! Look how my health has deteriorated, I can't meditate or spiritually evolve. I'm in a state of fear and panic every day to get the next bill paid so I don't get my phone or electricity turned off AGAIN! Look where I live and all the people around here. I don't mean to be judgmental, but it's not an enhancing environment to say the least! This city has the highest unemployment and crime rate per capita in the state.

Where you are is nothing. It is a trick your ego plays on you.

Well, I do believe that. But still . . . I do not have the strength, the invincibility of an enlightened person yet, since I am not. I am, unfortunately, affected from my environment, the collective consciousness of most people in the immediate area, not to mention certain circumstances that are in my life right now!

No, you are not. You give, give, give into the ego so easily Connie.

I know what that statement means, but what are you saying?

Connie, you believe what you have heard. That is not necessarily the truth. Why not decide to change your beliefs about that? You are a creator, after all. You have all the power to create that I do—that Jesus does—that God does. Let go of ego; the ego's limitations you believe. Smoke and be healthy—you can. Live in Daytona Beach and be full of joy—you can. You can live in poverty and be happy and at peace. You can create abundance. Do not accept the limitations the ego puts on you. You must talk to your ego like you do me. Instruct it. Tell it what you now know. It will succumb as you do. Speak to it now. Tell it what you believe. Do not allow it to tell you Connie.

I'm a little speechless. But, ok.

Talk to it now. What do you want it to know?

Well . . . I feel pretty ridiculous doing this, but I'll give it a try.

It is being a creator Connie, not a follower of the ego.

I did it. I told my ego I'm not a low-life and that I am capable and deserving of creating a great, happy, fulfilling life. But, I'm not going to go into more detail here because I'm too embarrassed to even write it down!

Yes, Connie. Now tell your ego this every day until you create it.

But, Babaji, do you know how ridiculous and unrealistic this sounds to me and most people?

Yes, that is why I'm here.

Thank you, Babaji. I feel daunted and defeated knowing how far I have to go to reach a higher level of perception, a higher level of awareness. I feel like I'm at elementary level and you are trying to teach me college level knowledge. It makes me feel so discouraged and hopeless.

When you are my child (student), you are so close. I will connect you to your God self. Just be willing.

I think your opinion of close may be different than mine, but ok. I am willing.

Yes, I know.

I'm depressed Babaji. I'm bored with my life. I'm lonely. I feel like it's going to take me many, many years or lifetimes to be enlightened—to be truly at peace and happy—to be with God.

You are much closer than lifetimes or many years away.

Feb 2, 2011

Babaji, I just read our conversations the last few days for the first time. I think I'm starting to understand more about what you've been saying and trying to teach. I'm starting to get that it is necessary to consciously intentionally recognize, acknowledge and intentionally feel whatever negative or disturbing thoughts or feelings one is having at the moment and feel them fully, without judging them, without resistance, without wishing them away.

To be alone and acknowledge what negative emotion one is presently feeling, whatever it is. Regardless of what one feels is the cause their pain, grief, worry, anger, etc., to not focus on the superficial issue they feel is the reason for their pain; to just feel the pain as deeply as they can—face it and fully feel it. When they do that, eventually they will free themselves of that pain, which is really caused from their ego's judgments, their beliefs, their perception about the issue, which was actually initially formed and created from a much younger age. Is that right?

Connie, you have just helped millions and millions of people by being willing to learn this from me and sharing it with others.

I know some people will read our conversations, but I seriously doubt it will be millions.

Limited Connie, limited Connie. You will catch up with my imagination as I said before.

You make me laugh Babaji.

Feb 3, 2011

Good morning Babaji.

Good morning Connie. Are you ready for the next lesson?

Yes.

Now it is time to allow something else. Need nothing more than what you have and everything will change to what you dream and desire to be manifested for you.

If I don't want something else, then I won't have dreams and desires for anything else?

I did not say want, I said need. There's a difference. Want, want, want, but do not need it.

Can you be more specific?

Yes. When you want something—better health, a new job or purpose, a soulmate, a family, a different situation, more material abundance, another car, anything, anything, anything—want it with passion, excitement and joy—dream, dream, dream. But, do not be dissatisfied, angry, disgruntled with not having it yet.

Being unhappy with the present moment as it is makes a hard, rough road to manifesting your dreams and desires. I will tell you why. When you have disgruntled, dissatisfied, unhappy feelings/energy within you, you will energetically attract more experiences that are in alignment with that same energy and bring you more of the same—disgruntled, dissatisified, unhappy feelings.

Like a magnet, you attract people and circumstances in your life that has the same quality of energy you have. You will not easily attract and create happier, more fulfilling experiences if you are not feeling happiness, joy or peace.

Yes, I understand that. The DVD and book, "The Secret" by Rhonda Byrnes talks about this. Esther Hick's books and videos talks about this. So does Dr. Wayne Dyer's books and videos. But how does one be happy and content with having what they don't want, like poor health, a job they hate, a car that is unreliable and disgusting, a life without an ideal or compatible partner, a life that they don't like, etc.?

I'm glad you asked Connie. You make a decision to not allow the ego to make you feel dissatisfied and unhappy without them. You make a choice that you are going to appreciate what do you have and be happy. Then and only then will you be able to manifest all you desire at the same time. Otherwise, you will always be dissatisfied and unhappy about something. You will struggle your way through trying to accomplish one thing at a time and never stop.

I understand what you are saying, but it seems next to impossible to do that!

It is impossible when you allow the ego to control your feelings. This is a lesson of conquering the ego. Remember, the ego can only exist through pain, dissatisfaction, displeasure, fear – that is its survival mechanism.

But can you explain more about how to just change your feelings like this?

Letting go of dissatisfaction is going to manifest satisfaction. And satisfaction creates peace and where there is peace, there is true power to manifest anything. This is what Eckart Tolle speaks of with being in the present moment—being in the present moment and accepting what is, without being in the past or future, which is where all dissatisfaction comes from.

Train your mind to be in the moment through accepting the present experience and do not forget that when dissatisfaction, pain, unhappiness arises, to spend time alone and face it. Feel it head on as deeply as you can and that pain, dissatisfaction or unhappiness will dissipate and eventually not exist. Then peace replaces it and creates.

Creates what?

Your passions, dreams and desires. Facing your dissatisfied, unhappy or painful feelings, without resisting them, will dissolve them away. Ignore them, resent them, resist them and they will always dominate and control your level of happiness and peace. Any kind of pain, in any form must be faced, felt fully and allowed to be, without guilt. Otherwise, your ego will continue to use it to keep you in that pain and then another pain and then another pain. Conquer the ego by facing it and feeling it fully, allowing it to be and then like magic, it dissolves away.

Thank you for pointing this out. I will remember this. But, any other specific advice on how to dissolve away any pain, dissatisfaction or unhappiness?

Yes. Face it, feel it fully and allow it to be there without judging it. Ignore nothing and you will succeed.

I'm presuming it might be ideal to give myself time alone to do this quite frequently then?

Yes. Do it every day. You will develop a new habit of allowing, of not resisting quickly.

That doesn't sound like much fun, but neither does the alternative—a lifetime of pain, dissatisfaction and unhappiness.

Believe me when I say you will transform this behavior of resistance quickly if you do.

I know when one meditates, is in silence and stills the mind regularly every day, that seems to automatically make one feel more peace, less stressed, less resistant to anything and everything and automatically seems to increase inner happiness regardless of life's circumstances changing or not. What do you think about this?

Yes Connie. Being in silence daily tames the mind, which pacifies and dissolves away the ego.

How and why does it have that effect?

When you silence the mind, the ego becomes passive.

Yes. I understand.

Feb 4, 2011

Babaji, I feel horrible.

Now for another lesson to learn. Do you know why you are feeling horrible?

Of course! I'm still smoking! Physically, I feel absolutely terrible and emotionally I am disappointed in myself and depressed with my life.

You have always been taught you needed to be a non-smoker to feel good and be healthy. Go beyond the ego Connie. That is such a pitiful limitation. You are not feeling terrible physically and emotionally depressed because you're still a smoker. You feel bad physically and emotionally because you "need" to be what you are not—a non-smoker. You believe you need to be a non-smoker to feel good physically and emotionally. You are judging it as bad. You feel shame and guilt about it.

Well, I guess I understand what you are saying. But, I think anyone would agree one is not going to be or feel very healthy if they're smoking.

Most people would agree, yes. Do you want most peoples' ego's limitations or my level of un-limitation?

Certainly yours.

Then train your mind to believe truth.

How do I do that?

Tell the ego it is wrong until you believe it.

Ok. But, I think I could tell my ego that ten times a day for the rest of my days and still not be able to believe that.

Want to believe that and you will. But, know your ego prefers these limitations. They make you feel terrible, weak, fearful. See yourself smoking and feeling incredibly healthy and happy.

Well, now that I think about it, I know of some people, Europeans in particular, that smoke, drink wine and eat bread and cheese every day, starting at lunchtime and they don't seem to have a problem with it at all! They feel just fine. They don't even think twice about it. I wish I could feel that way about smoking, but I just don't.

It is ideal to try to be healthy and not do things you know are unhealthy, but you can be a smoker and be perfectly healthy. It is your strong judgment about it that makes you feel so bad. Just be open to knowing these are ego limitations, not truth.

Ok Babaji.

Good.

If you were in a physical human body and smoked like a chimney, could you honestly be and feel totally healthy?

Yes Connie.

How?

Because nothing in the physical world has me fooled.

How have you been able to achieve this level of perception, this level of awareness?

From re-training my ego self's beliefs to my true self's knowledge.

Yes, I understand what you are saying. But, now I feel more discouraged than ever. I see just how far I have to go to conquer the ego. I feel I am at the beginning of learning this. I think it will likely take me many, many lifetimes of living with struggle and limitations until I do. It is so discouraging Babaji.

Yes Connie, I know. The ego loves to make you feel weak, fearful, helpless and discouraged. Laugh at it Connie and at least know it is wrong.

Ok Babaji.

All you need to do to know truth is to be willing to surrender your false beliefs. God does the rest.

Well, that makes me feel more encouraged, I guess.

Yes. You are learning much more than you realize right now.

I read in a book years ago that there have been some people— enlightened people that could drink poisonous snake venom and remain unaffected because they were able to transcend the limitations of the mind, of the ego. What do you think about this?

But, of course. Yes Connie.

Feb 5, 2011

Babaji, I'm so depressed, so numb with depression. I'm certainly not going to kill myself, but I feel so suicidal. I don't want to live anymore so badly I cannot tell you. I don't want to shower, to wake up every morning. I don't care about sex. I don't want to eat a full healthy meal now even if I could afford to and had the energy to make it. I do not want to wake up every day. I got my cell phone turned off yesterday, which is also my business phone. I was a few hours away from getting my electric turned off again a few days ago. I barely made rent, as usual. I know I've been having a busier couple weeks at work and I just got a new third job. Things are more hopeful now. But, I just can't take it anymore—struggling to survive like this.

I desperately need some nutraceuticals and I need to go to the doctor. I can't afford to as you know. I know if I just ate better, that would help more than anything, but I simply can't afford to. I've got such a nervous stomach all the time anyway from having so much stress and worries, I never have much of an appetite now anyway. I'm just too stressed. The pressures of getting one simple bill paid after the other is just too much.

I fantasize of the relief I would feel if I killed myself—the freedom and joy I would have if I didn't have to live anymore. It's getting even more unbearable. I think of others that may have it worse, but that does not help me feel any better.

You must feel your deep despair and depression Connie. You must intently feel it deeply or it will debilitate you even more.

That sounds sadistic to me right now! I'm tired of trying to feel worse and cry and sob. It's not going to change any of the circumstances in my life. It's not going to make me feel any better. If I need to keep living like this, doing this, I feel life and God is heartless, totally uncaring!

Yes, Connie. God cares, but cannot remove what you have created in your mind.

The only thing I have in my mind is a joyless life filled with too much financial burden, pressure, responsibility and very legitimate worries!

I've naturally been a happy person my whole life until I lost everything and have been living in poverty. I am working so many hours and I am exhausted. I can barely make it through each day. I need some money! That's what I need right now to feel better!

Connie, feel your despair, your lack of joy for life, your deep sorrow, your frustration.

Believe me, I already feel it! I just can't intently feel it deeper right now and try to focus on it more. I'm just not in the mood!

Connie, it will pass—this time, you will get through it.

How? By struggling through my life as usual, barely making it through each day? I don't want to continue putting one foot in front of the other continuously feeling physically horrible, exhausted, depressed, joyless and with this horrible underlying anxiety all the time. I hate my two second jobs. That means I hate almost every waking hour of my days and nights.

I know Connie. That's why you need to face it—fully. Not like a partial zombie each day. Feel it intently, solely and deeply and when you do—fully—it will disappear regardless of your physical and chemical make-up or the circumstances in your life.

I think any doctor would disagree with that theory.

I know Connie. I know.

I can do 'your work' AGAIN, feel my pain, but it's not going to change anything or change how I feel. I've been feeling all my varying feelings of misery. I feel worse, no better.

You will—if you continue till it's met fully.

Ok, maybe later. But, I just can't right now. I'm too numb.

Ok Connie.

I actually feel a little better just talking about it with you now though.

Yes. That's because you're starting to intently pay attention to it.

I think I'll do some laundry and clean up this house right now—AGAIN! If I could just have even a week off, I'd be so grateful. It's been many years since I've had even a short vacation. My life sucks! Living in poverty sucks!

Personal note: then I started crying for a few moments.

Connie, you did well.

If you're referring to getting so miserable and angry, I cried for a moment, I think that's going to make me infuriated with anger.

Yes. That is why I said you did well.

(smiling and chuckling) . . . I thought you might say that.

Now, do the laundry and clean the house.

I do feel a little better, a little lighter and brighter. I can actually smile just a little. I'm still not happy. But, I do feel a little better, not quite so overwhelmed.

Yes, Connie. We will get you through all of it.

Several minutes later . . .

I was just thinking about if I were a quadropalegic, blind or bed-ridden in major pain and agony as I used to be when I was mercury poisoned or with my back injury, how much I would have given to be in any other position; that if I were just not bedridden in such severe pain, I'd be the happiest most grateful person on earth. But, look at me now? I'm not happy at all. Why does thinking of this not make me feel better? I am very grateful I am not there anymore, but why doesn't it really make me feel happier or more at peace?

Because the ego has you fooled. Be happy with where you are and who you are. This time of living in poverty will change too and you'll still be unhappy until you conquer the ego.

For goodness sakes! How on earth do you conquer the ego!? Talk about a catch twenty-two! It's part of us, isn't it? It always will be, won't it? How on earth do we accomplish that?!

By meeting, facing and fully feeling all the pain it causes.

Feb 6, 2011

Hi Babaji.

Hello Connie. Have you not quit smoking?

No.

Why?

Because I don't want to deal with quitting!

Why?

Because it will bother me! I'm enjoying smoking right now, that's why!

Good Connie. I am so pleased you got to this point.

What?! That threw me for a loop!

Connie, I am pleased you are enjoying being a smoker now. Enjoy every moment of your life. When you are free of guilt about doing that, bad habits go away automatically.

I'm dumbfounded by your response.

Connie, please let go of your judgment, your guilt. It only serves ego. Free yourself by letting go of it.

You have me utterly speechless right now.

Yes. Now finish your computer work and then we can talk some more.

Ok.

Babaji, I'm miserable. I feel like a lion stuck in a cage. I feel trapped in a life I'm not supposed to be living. I want escape. I don't want to wake up tomorrow, as usual.

Why Connie?

Because I'm not going to be doing one single thing I want to do, that's why. I truly hate my two second jobs. They are so stressful and not good for me. I want to be living in a nice, roomy, clean organized house, not this sardine can where I'm living surrounded by boxes and clutter everywhere! I want to be in the mountains and in nature, have no money worries, have a refrigerator full of all the food I want, supplements I need, a new, nice enjoyable wardrobe, not dressed in a ratty pair of sweat pants as always.

I want to be able to relax, have fun and enjoy life for a change! Have a nice dinner out, look nice again, have no needs, no worries and a lovely home to go home to and a nice, clean smelling car again, like any of the ones I've had in the last 20 years before I had to trade my last car in for this total junker for the cash to pay my bills! I want to be free spirited, happy, healthy, able to enjoy and experience life in the moment again like I used to and continue to spiritually evolve.

Yes Connie. Why do you think you are not experiencing any of that now?

Because I'm broke because I had ten years of severe health issues! I lived off my savings all this time and spent over a million dollars in medical expenses my health insurance would not cover! Because I live in poverty now! Everything I do is just to struggle to survive!

Yes. Why do you think you're living in poverty?

Because I lost all my money and even though my back has gotten much better, I still have great limitations with what jobs I can get because of my back injury. I still can't sit much! I live in a poverty stricken area that doesn't have any jobs anyway!

No Connie. That is not why you're living in poverty with a back injury to cope with.

No?! Then why?

Because you needed to rid of the judgments you had about being all that you are now. It is time for you to evolve to Christ consciousness.

Babaji, I'm not really in the mood to hear that!

Connie, tell me what you've learned and accomplished from this experience; from living in poverty? You've already acknowledged this.

Yes, I know where you're getting at Babaji. I definitely have much more compassion and non-judgment than before. I feel I've always been a very caring and compassionate person toward others. I've always tried to be kind and polite to all people. But, until going through these last couple years of really struggling as I have been to such an extreme level, I realize that I did have some underlying judgments toward certain people that I was not consciously aware of before.

For example, I used to a have a level of negative judgment toward people that were not disciplined enough to take good care of their bodies and not have unhealthy habits like smoking or eating at fast food restaurants. Well, now I smoke and eat at fast food restaurants; I used to have judgment towards people that were overweight and simply wouldn't exercise even a few times a week. I've always been one to exercise almost every day whether I was in the mood or not. But, I haven't exercised in over a year now because I'm just too exhausted every day and I don't have the time or motivation to anyway. Now I'm overweight for the first time in my life because I've become hypo-thyroid due to being malnourished. I thought drug addicts or alcoholics were just weak people that used those substances as a cop out to deal with life effectively. I had judgment toward them. Well, now I drink alcohol regularly to help cope with all the stress from having such a stressful and unfulfilling life. I now have a lot of compassion for drug addicts and alcoholics. I can understand now that they probably had more challenging circumstances in their lives to cope with.

I used to judge people that kept their home a dirty, cluttered mess and didn't keep it at least tidy and somewhat well kept. Well, I've been living in a dirty, cluttered mess for two years now. I used to have judgment toward homeless people on the street. I honestly had compassion for them; I felt bad for them. I was always kind to them. In fact, I probably hold the world's record for buying more dinners for homeless people than anyone. I used to do that frequently.

But, I now realize that I did have some negative judgment toward them. I thought they were just lazy and incompetent; that all they needed to do was go out there and get a job and work hard. After all, that's what I did. I wasn't born with a silver spoon in my mouth. I worked 60+ hours a week the majority of my life from age 15 on until I was able to retire in my early thirties. Well, it took me forever to just get this third job; a measly minimum wage job that I'm well over-qualified for! I am literally on the verge of becoming homeless myself every month and I am not lazy and consider myself a competent person.

I used to have negative judgment toward people that didn't abide by the law with things like not paying their income taxes or driving with a suspended driver's license or without car insurance. I looked down on these people. I thought they were just blatantly irresponsible people that didn't manage their lives or money properly. Well, I got a speeding ticket several months ago that I simply could not afford to pay. My license got suspended as a result and I drove around in total paranoia for four months with a suspended license until I could finally afford to pay it. I drove without car insurance for six months. I haven't even filed my taxes in over a year! I've never not paid my taxes on time. Owning two businesses, I am not qualified to do my own taxes anymore and I have not been able to save a few hundred dollars to pay an accountant to file mine. I have knots in my stomach everyday afraid the IRS is going to be knocking on my door any moment. It's horrible!

I have become all of these people I now realize I did had some negative judgment toward. I think I may have unconsciously felt I was better than them in some way. I can honestly say, I do not think I could feel an ounce of negative judgment toward anyone on this planet. I have so much more compassion for these people and all people. I have such a deep desire to help improve people's lives in any way I can; to simply help them create more healing and happiness in their lives. My heart is filled with so much more love, compassion and non-judgment for all others. I guess I just need to let go of the judgments I may have for myself and I notice that I still have toward my father. I'm certainly trying to.

Feb 7, 2011

I'm so ugly now. My face looks so forlorn. I have horrible bags under my eyes. I look like I've aged 20 years in the last two years. I can't fit into any of my clothes anymore and I can't afford to buy any. It's embarrassing. I'm not even close to being in the shape I used to be in. I feel so pathetic, so miserable, so boring, so ugly, so low.

Connie, the only ugliness you see is your ego's thwarted perception. Oh, Connie, it is not real. Watch it play its tricks on you and laugh at it. Its only power is the belief you have in it. It is loving this moment of disgrace, of despair. Tell it you are facing it and laughing at it now. And laugh, laugh, laugh.

Laugh at it Connie. Allow it to play its games. Watch it play its games. Be entertained as you watch them with laughter. It's so weak, so fearful. Connie, it knows annihilation when it is near. Laugh, rejoice, laugh rejoice. I am here to the end Connie, to the beginning of Christ consciousness. Join with me fully Connie. Let go of all your fear.

I wish you were still in a physical body so I could hang out with you. I feel so alone in this world. I wish I had someone like you, a spiritual teacher in my life and I mean that's living in a physical body. I wish there were an ashram somewhere in this world that allowed doggies. If so, I would so love to live there for a while and put my time, attention and energy into being healthy and meditating and being able to live a life that's conducive to spiritually evolving. I wish I could be with you like some of your devotees were when you were here before.

Remove the veil in front of your eyes.

What do you mean?

You see cloudy Connie.

Yes, I know. What else can I do to see more clearly?

Feel your pain. Feel your judgments.

I'm tired of doing that. I've been doing more of that in the last few weeks than perhaps in my whole life. Can't I do something else?

Yes. Nothing.

Yes, nothing? What does that mean?

Yes, nothing, means yes, you can do something else—nothing.

I assume you're implying that nothing means, nothing helpful?

Yes Connie. The only way to salvation is through feeling your pain and feeling your judgments—fully.

Well, that's a big bummer.

Yes, it is a big bummer.

Several minutes later . . .

My life really sucks Babaji. I know it could always be worse, but nonetheless, it really does suck. How can I create a more enjoyable life? Well, I already know how to do that. It's having the lack of limitations that I need to have so I'm capable of doing things that are enjoyable. How can I have less limitations? And I hope you're not going to say, feel your pain, feel your judgments!

Connie, it is only your judgments that create limitations. Yes. Want more? Feel more.

Well, that's a bummer!

Yes, it is a bummer.

Well, I'm not in the mood to feel more crap right now! I'm going to save that for another day!

It's ok Connie. Enjoy what you can.

Thank you . . . I think?

Several minutes later . . .

I got my hair done today. First time in a year and a half! I'm resentful about that, but so appreciative and grateful at the same time.

Choose the latter Connie. It will serve you much better.

Yes, I know. But I can't believe I had to go over one and a half years without being able to afford a simple hair cut! That is incomprehensible! Unacceptable!

Yes, I know it is.

Well, you have me speechless again.

Listen to my mantra and feel my love instead.

Several minutes later . . .

There's a whole world out there to have fun and play in! And I'm stuck in this sardine can home in this depressed town and stressed out and bored working jobs I hate! Don't you think that's such a waste of life!

Yes, Connie. More than you are aware of.

Why won't you or God help me change my life for the better?! I feel so abandoned by God. I feel God doesn't love or care about me at all whatsoever! I feel utterly worthless.

Connie, it is time to reach your dharmic path and Christ consciousness. If your life were happy and fun right now, you would not be so strongly seeking God. This is a time to evolve to God awareness.

March 7, 2011

I barely know where to begin to catch up Babaji. I know we've had brief, un-recorded conversations, but there's a lot to catch up since I last had time to really speak to you. As you know, I've been extremely busy working with my clients and my two second jobs. It's been an exhausting, stressful time as you know. I wish I didn't have to work three jobs to barely make ends meet.

Connie, if you did not have this time of financial lack, you would not have gained what you have.

Well, I do understand what you're saying there. If I had plenty of money in the bank, I would not have been going through all of this, that's for sure. But, that would be to my great preference of course.

Connie, you have felt no pain in the last month. It is time to feel more pain.

Babaji, I'm really not in the mood to hear that. I'm too tired to do anything more.

Yes, I know. Release more pain and you'll feel more energy.

Maybe later Babaji. I'm not alone right now and I'm not up for it right now.

Ok. But, soon please. We have work to do.

What pain do I need to feel most right now, Babaji? I already feel so much pain from every single area of my life. What pain do you recommend I feel first? This is a serious question.

Which is the strongest?

I can definately pinpoint that one.

Good. Until you are ready to intently feel that, just listen more to my mantra.

Alright.

February 29, 2011

Babaji how does it feel to be so special with the unusual powers and abilities you have, being enlightened, having people at your feet, etc.?

My ego loves it. I still have an ego. But, I do not allow it to make my spirit self's awareness submissive to it. And my spirit self is always humble and in deep gratitude to our beloved Christ.

Did you get something a lot quicker than the average person or have you been around longer than the average person?

I got something quicker than the average person, yes. But, it still took me a very long time. The only thing that anyone can do that is presently un-enlightened, lacking the awareness of God, of your true self, is to allow the ego to make you feel anything it chooses. When you allow it, it has no more power; none. Stop ignoring or resisting it and you will save yourself many lifetimes of pain.

Accept feeling fearful, accept feeling depressed, accept feeling abandoned and betrayed by anyone, including God; accept being angry, accept being destroyed in your heart, accept being a destroyed heart and then Christ [consciousness] will enter it—

there will be no other place to go from there. Then you will experience fullness with our beloved Christ. Only a heart with full acceptance can accept Christ fully.

Let go Connie. Let go of your judgment. Watch your ego suck you back when you start progressing and opening your heart to Christ. It is so predictable. You do not notice how it plays its games. You are controlled by it continuously and you do not even know it. You are a leaf in the wind to your ego. Connie, become a storm and make that leaf go where you want it to. It is so easy.

You just ask Jesus to come heal your heart and I will do the rest from there. Whatever you need to overcome the ego, I will bring it to you. Connie, let go of your fear. Fear you cling onto easily. That is your biggest weakness your ego uses against you and you are as powerful as God. You are God. It is time to give in to your resistance. Let go of being an abused, pathetic, helpless, weak woman.

Your experiences are NOT who you are. You think you are your experiences, but you are not. Your identity is NOT a collection of your experiences. Your true self is underneath. Accept and you will see underneath.

Do you really want me to share all of these conversations with people? Even to prospective clients . . . people I don't even know?

Connie, free yourself. Yes. Not for me, for yourself. Why are you so reluctant to share our conversations to others? Because it is not professional? Because it is not ideal? Because it is not pretending to be fearless? It is not what you define as being perfect? Connie, let go of that child's play—baby, baby,

baby games. Move beyond that ridiculousness. You are not in kindergarten anymore. Be a leader, not a follower. Follow Christ and help lead the world to our beloved.

Personal note: the following conversation is with the spirit of a well—known enlightened spiritual saint that I briefly met once several years ago when I was ill with mercury poisoning. She is still living, so I do not feel it is appropriate to give her real name. She reminds me of what I imagine Mother Mary would be like, so I will call her Mary.

Mary, will you please talk to me? I feel like I'm missing something major!?

I am here Connie. You are not missing anything Connie. You are just learning the difference between fear and love as we all are. Connie, I will give you a little pointer that I know you are ready to accept. Love and nothing else. Love and nothing else. There will always be good reasons for not loving—so many good reasons. The reasons do not matter. Love regardless. When you need to be justified to love, it is not love. Have no good reason to love and love anyway. Then, you'll need no more lack of love in your life. Connie, we will be meeting soon.

We met once before, but this is beyond the physical meeting. Christ, our savior is waiting for you. Connie, remember when we embraced (she hugged me when I met her)? I knew this day was coming when you would be talking to me now and be our Jesus' follower as a healer and here you are now—as a healer, not as a victim.

Connie, be brave now. The ego is most strong now. The only way to conquer it is to allow it like Babaji said. When you are feeling hateful, angry and fearful—feel it. Do Babaji's Work. You must

Connie, otherwise you will delay. And, Jesus is waiting for you. I said a prayer for your growth to Jesus.

Mary, I don't care about anything else in my life anymore. Not about marriage, having children, being in great shape again, nice clothes, a nice home, a sex life, having friends. I don't think this is very healthy or good. It is disconcerting to me. But, really I do not care much about anything but being with Jesus, Babaji and God anymore. I care of nothing else.

Connie, it is natural to eventually care only about God. But the main point to address is that you will never feel God until you accept the ego's fullness of 'no good'. Ironic, isn't it? Be strong Connie and when you have a reason to hate, to be angry, to feel abandoned, know that you are justified and let it go. The ego will hang onto needing to be justified. Know in advance you are already legitimately justified. Not as a trick, as a truth. Justification makes the ego strong. Know this in advance and need no justification. You want to surrender your pain, not to strengthen it.

Jesus, what do I need to do to surrender my pain and fears? I am aggravated to hear what Babaji just said. You must know I want nothing more than You and God! How on earth do I surrender? How do I let go? You know I am truly willing to do anything, I just don't know how. Please tell me something else, something more. Exactly how do I let go and surrender to you?

Do Babaji's work. You just said you would do anything but you are not doing Babaji's Work. Do it every day until we are one. It is only your pain that separates us. You keep ignoring Babaji's work. Do Babaji's Work and heal the pain you created. Your pain is all yours and belongs to no one else. Ignoring it will not make it go away. Only by facing it, feeling and accepting it will it go away. It is there because you are resisting love. Resisting love is resisting me, personally. What do you fear the most? What do you hate the most? Be that, feel that, experience that, face that and all that separates you from me will be dissolved. Keep procrastinating and you will wait. Connie, you have been given all you need to be with me. You resist it. It is not involuntary, your resisting me. It is voluntary.

Jesus, forgive me for saying this but you sound like you're not being very understanding or compassionate. You make it sound like I could simply snap my fingers and surrender whatever I need in order to unite with you. What am I missing?

The only thing you're missing is doing Babaji's Work.

Jesus, for one thing I am literally too busy trying to earn a living and survive in this material world. But, regardless, I'm tired of feeling my depression, anger, unhappiness, disappointment, etc.! I can hardly believe you are telling me I have not felt enough pain in various forms from my life?!

I'm not trying to compete with other people's challenges or painful experiences. But, I honestly feel the experiences I've been given in this one lifetime are far beyond the average person's level of painful experiences. Although, I'm sure many people may feel this way about their lives.

What on earth do you and God want from me? Seriously. I've given everything I know. My biggest and deepest desire since I was 21 years old and started meditating was to be able to live a life where I can focus on evolving spiritually. I've obviously surrendered everything! If I haven't voluntarily surrendered it, I've been forced to. I have nothing left anymore. I have nothing left in me to give . . . materially, physically, emotionally or spiritually. Can you not see I have nothing to give anymore?

I'm not implying I'm a saint or a Mother Theresa. But I feel I've given my whole life to the point I have nothing to give to anyone, including myself. What more can I do?

Connie, do Babaji's Work and heal the pain you have created. There is no other way to receive God's grace. Let go Connie. Let go of it and the need to feel it is unnecessary.

Babaji, I know from what you said before that the source of all pain is from having a lack of God awareness, of our true selves; feeling separate from God. But what are the specific and practical reasons that I am so depressed, lonely, empty, lost, so displaced in this world, in my existence?

Connie, you are resisting love. There is no other answer I can give you that is more accurate.

Precisely, how am I resisting love?

You are not accepting being your true self Connie. You are not healed, you are not strong and you are not courageous. You let your experiences own you. You did not accept them and learn from them without letting them change who you are in your perception of yourself, as most people do. Your perception is your reality. You are not your true self. You gave into the ego. Now, the ego owns you, quite literally. You are lost, empty, depressed because your true self is not predominating over the identity your ego has given you.

And, guess what that identity is? It is your biggest fears and dislikes. Your ego always wants you to experience your biggest fears and dislikes. And you believe you are that now. You are *not* weak or helpless. You are not what you judge. You have owned it but you are still not that. You *are* in control of your life. You *are* strong and courageous. You are not helpless. You are a powerful creator.

You know what you want to be but you do not create it because you have accepted all but what you are. You could be your true self tomorrow, Connie—as of this very moment. You want to be a healthy person? Let go of your judgments about having bad habits and not being a person that takes good care of their body. Then your ego will not need you to have bad habits and not take good care of your body.

Force yourself to quit with effort and resistance and it will find another way to make you unhealthy because you judge it so negatively. It is your judgments that create your reality. Release the negative judgments and replace them with love. That is your true self. You judge living in poverty with negative judgment? You will eventually live in poverty. You were successful at a relatively young age. You were financially set for life. Why did you lose it all? Because you became so ill you lost all your money to health issues and expenses.

What else do you negatively judge, Connie? Having a boyfriend that is not financially stable? Now you have a boyfriend that is not financially stable after a lifetime of having successful boyfriends and partners. Negatively judge living in a place like Daytona Beach? Well, now you live in Daytona Beach instead of beautiful Palm Beach.

What else? You will eventually become it, experience it until the judgment against it is released. How do you surrender these negative judgments? Accept being them. You are not unhappy because you are experiencing all your fears and judgments. You are unhappy because you are still negatively judging them. You need only to accept them with love, compassion and forgiveness.

Forgive yourself for having bad habits. Forgive God for the ten years of health issues you had that now has you penniless and living in poverty. Forgive your boyfriend for living in Daytona. Forgive your father for not loving you enough. Forgive your mother for not loving herself enough. Do "my work". Feel and honor the pain in your heart. Save yourself from needing these painful, unwanted, unnecessary experiences to achieve self-awareness. Help save others from doing the same by sharing our conversations.

Personal note: I want to briefly address something miraculous. Babaji never told me this was going to happen. A few weeks after I started doing Babaji's Work nearly every day, my back injury that I had been coping with for many years began to improve DRAMATICALLY! The level of pain I was in everyday and the inability I had to sit for much more than an hour at a time, greatly improved. This is one of the biggest blessings of my life! To this present day, in February, 2013, this improvement has remained.

Summary of Babaji's Work

Word for word from Babaji:

Be alone, be comfortable. Think of what you are mostly distressed about right now. What is bothering you the most right now? Put your attention on one issue at a time. Start with the most bothersome issue.

Now that you have the most bothersome issue acknowledged, how is it making you feel? Think about your feelings now; not the issue, not about how valid you are for feeling the way you do. Do not think you are bad, wrong or weak for feeling the way you do. Do not judge yourself. Do not judge the person or situation that has you feeling as you are. What are you feeling most now from this issue? Identify the emotion. Name it.

Fearful, worried, inadequate, anger, resentment, jealousy, sorrow, regret, resentment, frustration, shame, guilt, helpless, hopeless, unloved, unwanted, uncared about, ugly, undesirable, lonely, empty, lost, confused, afraid, nervous, insecure, cowardly, abused, victimized, abandoned, betrayed, humiliated, devastated, hateful toward someone, toward God, toward Jesus, toward me, toward yourself, unappreciated, not good enough, unworthy, completely worthless, stupid, pathetic, sick, overwhelmed, insane?

Identify which feeling is the strongest. Listen to a song that repeats my mantra. Now honor this feeling by giving it your sole attention. Sit or lay there undistracted and try to feel this particular feeling. Do not think about why you feel this feeling. You are already justified for having this feeling. You are genuinely validated for feeling this feeling. Now feel it—intently. Feel how deep this pain is. Ignore nothing. Just feel it.

If you are having trouble feeling it more deeply or trouble feeling anything, think back to a memory of when you felt this same or similar feeling. Think of some experience that made you feel bad in a similar way—hurt, fearful, angry, etc. Think back to that time, that experience and feel what you felt then. Feel it intently, as deeply as you can. If you are able to feel this feeling intensely, stay with it until it subsides naturally; lessens and lightens and you now feel ready to get back to your day.

Do this every day at least once. Do it more often as you would like. You cannot overdo this, but keep each session under an hour. Some may naturally feel finished within a few minutes, sometimes longer. Some days you will be able to experience the feeling more deeply, other times, less so. Accept whatever comes. Allow whatever comes and know it will pass. Know it is only a feeling. The feeling itself cannot hurt you. The feeling will not kill you. But the resisting of it can. When you do this, you are not resisting it; you are facing and honoring it. This is what will free you from all your pain, all your fears, all your judgments. This will bring you to God's feet—the place you need to reach to surrender to our Beloved Christ—to surrender to God with total love, compassion and non-judgment.

Do not be afraid to feel—ever. Negative feelings are merely feelings. They are illusions, but very real to you now. You will come to know they are illusions only by facing and feeling them—giving them your attention—honoring them. Their power over you will quickly diminish. Soon, you will be able to laugh at them when they arise. You will know they are not you. You will know they are not real. They are harmless, meaningless, insignificant. Then your power of God, of love, will begin to expand in ways you cannot imagine.

When you begin again, start with the beginning of this summary. Doing this every day will free you quickly. Listen to my mantra in a song when you are doing this if you can. If you cannot, repeat it silently in your mind or out loud for ten minutes or more before beginning.

Then pour your heart out to Christ and our Father. This means feel your love and devotion to Them. Simply honor Them and ask Them for union.

Additional note: The exact pronunciation of my mantra, *"Om Namah Shivaya"* is not important. But, Connie will display the typical pronunciation of my mantra. Remember its meaning:

"I surrender to you God" **or** *"Lord, Thy will be done"* **or** *"I bow/ surrender to my higher inner self"*. It is intentionally asking God (love) to awaken you—to expand within. Repetition of my mantra directly changes your DNA to that of someone who is fully awakened. It releases your pain and fears more effectively than anything else ever has or ever will.

Om Na-mah Shee-vi-ya

I asked Babaji to give a more condensed summary of "His work" for quick referencing.

Brief Summary of Babaji's Work

1. Be Alone. Be comfortable.
2. Think about what is disturbing you the most today, or at this time.
3. Define what the feeling is; do not think about it.
4. Know you are justified and validated for feeling this.
5. Listen to my mantra or repeat it silently or out loud, for about ten minutes or as long as you like.
6. Intentionally feel this feeling as deeply as you can. Do not judge it, just feel it.
7. When the feeling subsides naturally, get back to your day.
8. If you have trouble feeling deeply or identifying any feeling, remember a past experience that caused you to feel a similar way. Or, think of any memory that caused you pain. Then remember the feeling of this pain and feel it as deeply as you can.
9. Do at least one session every day. Feel each and every pain in your heart. Do this with every painful memory you have. Do this until they are gone.
10. Then you will be at the one pain you have left to heal—the pain from the loss of God. Feel this pain and you will then be set free. Ask God for union—for wholeness with yourself, for wholeness with all.

You can heal the pain in your heart this way or by going through numerous "real" painful events in your life. Until you acknowledge, face and feel them all, they remain with you. Honor them now (in your mind and in your heart) without needing the actual experiences to accomplish this. This is the quicker, easier path to Christ consciousness.

You will heal them quickly if you are willing. If unwilling, you will heal them slowly.

Om Na-mah Shee-vi-ya

Questions and Answers
with Jesus

December 2012

The Bible says "As you sow, so shall you reap". I think that describes karma. Does karma really exist? If so would you please explain it?

Yes, karma does exist. Some misunderstand it as being a delivery system for punishment. There is no such thing as punishment from me or God. Karma is a natural process that occurs in life. Whatever energy you give out from your thoughts, feelings or actions does eventually return to you, the sender. It is simply a causeway of action to reaction. People believe punishment is necessary when they are fear-based and filled with guilt and shame.

What about people that do dreadful acts? People that are harmful to society? Rapists, thieves, murderers, abusers—what do we do about them?

Removing them from society is logical. Until they are more healed, they should be removed from society so they do not continue to cause harm. But, how they are treated when in jails and prisons is what needs to be addressed. You may not want to hear that giving them love and compassion is what they need. Yet, it is what they need. Treat them with kindness and compassion. Help them heal. Do not give them more of what created their unloving behavior in the first place. That will never help them. That will never rehabilitate them. That will never help society. Enable them to live healthy, happy, balanced lives within a contained society until they are balanced—healed and balanced. Also, give them this book.

Does reincarnation for humans really exist?

Yes, it does. When the physical body dies, your spirit always eventually moves forward toward another physical existence. The physical body comes to an end, of course. Yet your true Self never dies. The spiritual being of who you are wants to continue being reborn in order to experience more.

Before you were born you were pure consciousness, pure love energy—God. Your physical existence enables you to experience and express the love that you are. Being love is *being* love. But *experiencing* love is a different aspect of existence. It includes the ability to experience and express love. This is a most beautiful, joyous and fun existence.

Eventually you become fully aware of your God Self. Yet you will still continue with the process of living as human beings in order to again experience the love that you are.

I thought that when one eventually becomes fully enlightened, they are not then reborn into the physical—that they go to "heaven" and are united with God for all eternity in the non-physical. Why would one want to be reborn again if fully enlightened?

You talk like it is a punishment to exist and I understand why. But, later you will understand how nothing compares to experiencing being who you are in a physical reality. Experiencing with the full awareness of who you are—pure love. God energy is the most incredible experience you could imagine. In the non-physical form you are **being** love. In the physical form you **experience** being love. It gives you the opportunity to express the love that you are, not just be who you are. It is ecstatic, fun and joyful. You will continue reincarnating on earth until every person is fully enlightened. Then you will still continue reincarnating on earth.

What exactly are angels? Do we all have angels? What are they here for? What do they do?

Yes, angels have always existed since humans and they always will. Angels are spiritual beings that are with humans to help them grow and evolve. Angels support the coordination of the collective consciousness created by all humans in order to support your individual needs and desires. Angels instill their specific area of expertise to those that need it.

Everyone always has angels. They are your non-physical best friends. Talk to them. They can support you more when you ask them for assistance. Some angels come and go as needed, some stay with you from birth and on throughout your life.

Is there such a thing as an evil angel? Is there such a being as "Satan" or the "Devil"?

There is always the opposite of everything in the existence of a physical world. There has to be. You could not experience love in the physical without also knowing its' opposite. You could not experience what you consider to be good, if there were not the opposite of that. You could not experience hot without the existence of cold. And one cannot appreciate beauty without an idea of ugliness.

Yes there is a devil, too. It is a being that is fully lacking in love and compassion. And, it is lacking to the exact level of the presence of love and compassion of Me. Always, there is the exact same level of an opposite in your existence.

All will attract angels that are in alignment with their level of consciousness. One attracts angels both consciously (asked for) and unconsciously. If you desire negative, lower level of consciousness angels, you will attract them. If you desire loving, compassionate angels, you will attract loving, compassionate angels. You consciously and unconsciously attract angels. Some come automatically to help support you when needed, some come when you specifically ask for them. This goes for higher evolved or lower evolved angels.

Can negative, lower evolved, evil angels come to us if we don't want them to? If we don't consciously ask for or want them to?

Yes, but it is rare. When this occurs, it is always a reaction of energy you gave out sometime before. You will eventually learn what is needed from all experiences that are painful—how to overcome your judgments, how to love more. When you love as fully as I do, as fully enlightened people do, you never need to experience any form of pain again.

What would you recommend someone do if they have an unwanted "evil angel" with them—if they are aware of it anyway?

Pray to God to heal your fear. All pain and suffering comes from your own fear, not from God. Face your fear as deeply as you can. Accept it. Do Babaji's Work.

Is it natural to sometimes have illness? Is it just a part of being human? Is there an underlying source that is the cause of all illnesses?

It is not natural to have illness, no. The source of all illness comes from not being fully loving. All forms of imbalances in your existence come from not being fully loving. Fear manifests into all dysfunctions. Do Babaji's Work and heal your pain. This will dissolve your fear.

Much is being reported this year about violence, gun crimes and mass shootings. Would you please comment about this and related issues?

Yes. When people do not live a balanced life, they become stressed—overly stressed. They do not care as well. They do not care for themselves well, their children or others; they become fearful, angry, perturbed, unhappy and irritated and they behave differently as a result. As you can see everyone's feelings and their actions that follow affect everyone else. Many other people are also directly affected by a shooter's actions. If you do not improve the quality of your lives—such as being healthier, happier, more balanced, experiencing more joy and less stress, the result will continue and progress.

There is also so much "childhood bullying" these days. There are more and more cases of children being so mean-spirited and even violent. It is horrible. Any suggestions about this?

Yes. Support living a more balanced life. It is the same answer Connie. Adults are becoming more fearful and violent. Children are becoming more fearful and violent. When one becomes more stressed, they behave differently. It is as simple as that.

There's supposedly a "good reason", a gift from every challenging experience. Is this true?

Yes. The gift in any challenging experience is being given the opportunity to surrender your pain, your fear. Once you face and fully feel all the illusions of separation created by ego, there is no such thing as pain, suffering or fear. All challenging, painful experiences are there to enable you to have more love, compassion and non-judgment—to expand awareness of your spirit self. You do this by learning how to accept and surrender your pain.

I heard on the news about a man that was cruelly imprisoned in another country. It seems such an unfair and horrible experience. Why did this happen to him?

He had a past experience where he was abandoned and having had that experience, he manifested a fear of abandonment. Over several different lifetimes of this, his fear of abandonment strengthened and created another deeper experience of abandonment. Once you have formed a new fear, it will manifest as an experience that is in alignment with that fear energy. It has strengthened over several lifetimes and is now becoming a most extreme case of being abandoned.

He will continue to unconsciously create such experiences until he surrenders that fear. When he surrenders that fear of abandonment, he will no longer have the fear and will no longer create situations of being abandoned. Every emotion you have, good, bad or indifferent, creates and manifests your experiences. All experiences are created from your emotions and you are never "neutral", feeling nothing. You are always feeling, creating something.

You make it sound like we take our fears with us from lifetime to lifetime. They are NOT wiped clean in each new lifetime? Is it then destiny that we must keep unconsciously creating and re-creating fearful and painful circumstances, sort of like "Ground Hog Day?

Your pain and fears are not wiped clean with a new lifetime, no. You take them with you. You will not have the memory of why they are there from your previous life's experiences of course, but they remain within you until they are healed. Until you do Babaji's Work on them. You must do Babaji's Work to free yourself from all pain—all your fears that are there as a result of your pain. Babaji's Work is needed to become free of your fears.

What could all of us Americans learn from the experience of that man's unjust captivity?

I would recommend that all Americans and all other nations learn to be more loving, kind, caring and compassionate to others. If someone that had the logistical ability to help that imprisoned man, cared enough, had enough compassion, he would not have been there as long as he was. If the people that took him had enough compassion, they would not have taken him in the first place. You increase your ability to have more love and compassion when you expand spirit and heal the pain in your heart.

Some people did have the logistical power and ability to help him. Their response was "there was nothing they could do to help free him". What do you say to that?

I would suggest they do what they would do if he were one of their beloved.

Regarding that one particular captive, what is happening to the USA, the once most powerful country in the world—that they cannot protect their American citizens, demand and achieve the release of an American citizen?

You (America) are losing your strength and power because you have not been able to grow and evolve anymore. The table is now going to dramatically shift from being one of the most respected, powerful, influential and ideal countries to live in, to the extreme opposite. It worked. America's principles did work—before. Obviously, America became powerful, abundant and "ideal" in many ways. What was being practiced and done by America's government and America's citizens worked. Can you see that?

Things changed along the way and are not working now. What has changed? That is the question to ask. What has changed to now make America less powerful, less abundant and less influential? The main answer to that question is the citizenry not living a balanced life. People are too stressed. This manifests differently for each person. But, the more stressed one is, the more irritated they become; agitated, fearful, angry, greedy, unhappy, sad and depressed. All of these feelings result in specific behaviors and create the same—more fear, more sadness, more illness, more anger, more insecurity . . . and that is the main answer to this question.

The culture would do better to support living a balanced life. That is, a balanced level of time spent enjoying life, balanced time spent working, balanced time with loving relationships, balanced time spent with oneself. If you are often exhausted, usually unhappy, too busy, too imbalanced, you are not in a "good place" so you will not attract or create "good" things. The question now should be; how do you get out of this situation of living in major discord, disharmony and imbalance? You first have to become more desirous of having a balanced life than in maintaining the imbalanced lives the majority of you have created.

Is it really possible to end poverty? If so, how?

The only way to end poverty is to care enough to not permit it. That requires expanding spirit, expanding your level of awareness, your level of consciousness to becoming more of who you really are—loving God energy. That being said, there are many different ways each person can help others improve the quality of their lives. Throughout your own life, make it a habit to help whoever comes your way, whenever you can. Seek others, that is be alert to the opportunity of noticing others that have a need for help and care enough to give help in whatever way you can.

Do we just give people what they need or is it better to try to help them become capable of meeting their own needs?

Do both. Give to others what they need in the moment if you comfortably can and help them obtain the knowledge, the opportunity or whatever is needed to attain self-sufficiency, better health, more happiness, etc.

How do we keep the faith and an open heart during challenging times in life?

You accept the challenging situation as it is. This is the only correct answer to that question. There are other helpful hints but, that is the only way to have peace through challenging times.

Acceptance goes against the ego's ways. The ego is against everything, good or bad. Its very nature is to resist whatever exists, good and bad and to cause more conflict, more pain, more dissatisfaction, more suffering, more separation and more fear and the ego will always be this way. You disempower the ego when you accept whatever "is" through each moment. Now, how do you accept a very unacceptable, challenging situation? You learn balance. Balance between acceptance and balance between doing what you can to improve a situation to your liking.

Write down a problem(s) in front of you. This will help make it clear and put it in perspective and make visible a solution more efficiently. Write down what you feel is reasonable and logical to help correct or improve the problem. Follow with the action that you would take and accept it at the same time as much as you can throughout and during the challenging experience.

Surrender is the tool that enables you to accept. Surrender your problem to me, doing what you can along the way but leaving it to God to bring help, assistance, a miracle. Those who can surrender more effectively can accept whatever exists more effectively, and will experience more peace through challenging times.

So, after doing Babaji's Work, you suggest we surrender our resistance, pain or challenging situation to you?

Yes. Do Babaji's Work and then surrender it to me. This is the most significant thing you can do to increase your happiness, peace and improve your health. As well as the recommendations I discussed to enhance evolving spiritually [in message #3].

What if someone doesn't believe in you, Jesus, yet still wants to surrender?

Surrender them to God. I am love, compassion and non-judgment. You will have to surrender them to love, compassion and non-judgment. That is what heals any pain.

How would you suggest parents handle children with a terminal illness?

Write down on a piece of paper what can help their child and all others involved to be more comfortable and improve anything in anyway. Accept that their child is going to die and surrender their resistance to God with trust and faith knowing it is something beyond their control and surrender that to God.

I am sorry Jesus, but that answer seems so trite. Easy to say "just surrender". But I think the loss of one's child is HUGE. And to tell a parent to just "accept and surrender falls" quite short.

It is quite insufficient. It is incredibly insufficient. Until you are enlightened—that is, until you have the full awareness of who you really are—God and united with all, separation becomes a part of your life. That is why I am speaking to you now Connie. That is why I am asking you to share my messages to the world.

It is time to end all pain, separation and fear on earth. The world is ready for these messages.

Why do we not remember our prior lifetimes?

You could not handle the knowing of being immortal. Your consciousness is not at a level where you can handle that knowing and the nervous system of your physical bodies could not handle all the love and all of the pain experienced from all lifetimes. If you remembered all the bad experiences, you would not be able to handle it. This also includes all the love experiences. You need to start from scratch again and gradually increase awareness so you can withstand the expansion of love energy.

When you are born your memory is new. You start out with a fresh clean slate. That gives you the opportunity to increase your level of awareness. Each lifetime, you gain the ability to love more. The painful memories are wiped free, but the ability to love fuller and deeper remains with you. When you are enlightened, you are completely filled with love energy and you do not judge at all as you do now. What you call "bad or painful" experiences would not be judged as bad. Until you are free of fear, you are not going to be free of judgment. Having the memory of all your past lives would be too overwhelming for you.

Why can't we be like animals and just enjoy life without having an egoic perception? Animals are naturally "in the present moment". Their existence seems much happier and more at peace than most humans. Their minds are free from worry. Some mammals, such as dogs always love automatically. They do not harbor resentments. Is there something good or advantageous from having an ego perception?

Yes. The ability to love is possible only when you have the opposite of love. You are able to experience more examples, billions of examples of experiences of expressing the love that you are. Without an ego there would be no identity of "you" and "you" would *be* nothing but love, not *experiencing* love as you are able to in a physical reality, as a physical being.

Bad experiences are only bad because you judge them as bad. They are just a different manifestation as God's love energy in many different forms. I see all forms as beautiful expressions of God's loving energy. Judgment is what brings suffering, not the ego—the perception and the judgment. That is what brings disharmony, discord and suffering.

Not all, but some of the deceased loved ones I've communicated with seem to be able to experience love in their existence, but without pain and they still seem to continue to evolve. They seem completely detached and not in any pain.

It is easier until you become both—physical beings with awareness of your spirit self as one. They do not experience physical experience. You are able to experience the physical aspects in physical bodies. Your goal is to have your spirit fully expanded; to be fully aware of your spirit self while still in your physical body. When you become pained enough, you begin seeking God and start on a "spiritual path", with a stronger desire to spiritually evolve. When you do, you become detached as your deceased loved ones sometimes are, but also in your physical body in the physical world. It is a beautiful experience you all wanted. That is why you reincarnate to again experience life in a physical existence.

What do you see coming up for the year 2013? Any particular advice for people in this upcoming year?

2013 is a new beginning of a new era. It is a new phase on earth and it is going to be a phase where people basically go one way or the other. Meaning, evolve spiritually, expand heart or not. You will need to expand spirit and expand heart. They are one and the same.

In order to remain living on earth, those who are not open enough, desirous enough to expand spirit will become more and more uncomfortable in many different ways—financially, health or inner turmoil for no apparent reason; or more obstacles and problems in one form or another. You will continue to become more uncomfortable. These obstacles or moments of increased discomfort are opportunities to turn away from what is upsetting, caused by your judgments and turn toward expanding spirit and heart instead.

Those who continue loving will be accepted to move forward and stay here on earth. Those who choose not to expand spirit will not be accepted to stay on earth. They will be moving to another physical existence elsewhere. It will be filled with nothing but people who are unable to expand spirit now. They will need more intense fearful experiences to be capable of expanding spirit. And earth is not going to be able to support the experiences those people need. Earth is ready to evolve because enough people on earth are ready to evolve. The scale has finally tipped.

After the end of a several year period of time that has now just begun, the people remaining on earth will all be people who are open and desirous enough to expand spirit and all will then evolve extremely rapidly—very quickly.

Another word of advice for this year is to be able to effectively notice your judgments. It is a critical year for understanding that judgments are not helpful to you. If one can understand the meaning of judgment, the reason for judgment, the insanity of judgment just a little more, then you will be able to expand spirit enough this year to change your destiny in the direction you are in now to a much better outcome, a much easier path.

So pay attention to this one thing alone—become aware of judgments; what they are, when you judge, why you judge. This is why I am asking you to share these messages now. Judgment, judgment, judgment. It is the main topic of discussion. It will surpass everything else automatically if you learn a little more about judgment and how it brings you more pain and suffering.

What do you mean by "be accepted"? Who will accept or not accept people on earth?

This will be hard for you to understand. The answer is yourselves. But I will further elaborate. Your spirit self, everyone's spirit self, knows what you need to become more aware of your spirit self and will bring you the experiences you need when you are ready. There are some people at level A, let's put it that way. Level A wants to evolve spiritually. Some people are in the middle, level B. They will be influenced one way or the other. Level C is people stuck in a rut—not close to being ready to evolve spiritually.

Earth now has more people ready to, wanting to evolve spiritually than not. So, this earth is going to evolve with the people. The people in level C will not be able to evolve here, so they will need a different place to go, literally. They will not fit in on earth staying stuck without evolving. Therefore, they will need to go elsewhere where they can have the experiences they need to enable them to continue evolving spiritually. Earth is not going to be able to accommodate those people's needed experiences.

A word of advice for this year would be to save the unnecessary disruption and start expanding spirit now. Do not wait longer. It will only get more uncomfortable if you do not start putting your attention, desire and some energy toward spiritually evolving. Message #3 discusses several ways to evolve spiritually. Babaji's Work needs to be given to the world, Connie. It is the be-all end-all to suffering and pain; to healing the heart. A healed heart is an expanded spirit. They are one and the same.

What about the people that want to evolve spiritually but cannot live a life that is conducive for evolving spiritually because they are struggling just to survive?

They will be able to when they have a more healed heart. They are in a time of more struggles because they are healing their heart—a phase that occurs when needed. Acceptance and surrender is all you can do during most trying times.

How does going through more struggles heal the heart? One's heart is hurting more during a time of more struggles, not less.

When you are feeling deep pain—when your heart is in deep pain, deep fear, you are releasing the pain and fear that is already present. Feeling the pain that is already in your heart from past experiences releases them; it frees you of your pain and creates a more healed heart as a result. A more healed heart is capable of loving more. That is why doing Babaji's Work is needed. When doing Babaji's Work, you learn how to heal your heart *without needing the challenging experience.*

But, you have <u>more</u> of a broken heart when going through a very challenging time, don't you?

A broken heart is needed to impel you to let go and let God.

Why is a broken heart needed to "let go and let God"?

One does not usually surrender until they are so broken that they give in. But you *can* accept and surrender without having a broken heart to spiritually evolve. When you go through a more difficult time in life, you need to evolve more. The need to evolve more is what brought (attracted) the difficult experience. You can evolve more through healing your heart. Feeling the pain in your heart induces letting go of more of your fears. Surrendering more of your fears occurs when you feel more pain and then the capacity to love more increases.

Doing Babaji's Work prevents you from attracting further painful experiences. No one can avoid the need to heal one's pain. Doing Babaji's Work—intentionally feeling the pain that is already present in your heart—is a quicker, easier path to achieving God consciousness. Babaji's Work will save you lifetimes of unnecessary, painful experiences.

Some people have no interest in or desire to "spiritually evolve", but are kind, compassionate and loving people. They try to spread kindness, caring. What about them?

It all depends on the level of their ability to love. It will vary from person to person. Expanding spirit intentionally is most effective. But, when someone is more love than fear and is increasing their love, yet does not meditate or consciously expand spirit, they will still be expanding spirit anyway. *Loving more is the same as expanding spirit*. You do not have to meditate or say "I am evolving spiritually" to expand spirit, no. Love enough. That is all that is needed.

When you were here on earth as a human being, were you just a fully enlightened man or were you different than every other human being?

I was different. Everyone is different and unique, yes. But, I was a different quality of a human being than all other human beings. This quality is a quality that is hard to explain, but I will. God energy formed me into a physical form for one purpose—to save all the people on earth from declining to self-destruction.

All of you are as much of a manifestation of God energy as I am. I was created as a physical manifestation of God as you all are, but was capable of loving beyond the level of love that existed at that time. I enabled all humans on earth to be capable of loving to a higher capacity, because I created it first. Basically, I was given the ability to love more quickly than every other human. I was able to evolve much quicker to save the world from self-destruction. This will not be able to be fully understood with the mind, but it is a good generalized answer. Yes, I was a different quality of human being, but I was still a human being.

What do you mean a different quality of a human being—still human, but different? Can you explain further?

This quality enabled me to love to a much fuller, deeper level than ever before. You all will be able to love to my capacity—

the same level and depth of loving. This is because I initially created the ability to love much more. I was the same as all other humans but simply put, I had the ability to evolve much quicker. This was for one purpose: to help save the world from self-destruction.

But, what was different about you that enabled you to love more fully and evolve much quicker? What exactly was different about you from other humans?

I was not given any past experiences from prior lifetimes. It was my only life as a human being—in a physical form. All of you had many previous lifetimes and I had no previous lifetimes. That is what enabled me to love much fuller, deeper and quicker.

Everyone has had an original, first lifetime, yes? Why were we not capable of loving and evolving like you?

I was not born as a human being to evolve and experience life. I was born only to help all the people on earth from destroying themselves.

How/why were they going to destroy themselves?

They had too much fear. When you become too fearful, you self-destruct, literally. You destroy yourself, you destroy others and others destroy you. They could not love enough because their fear became so powerful and overwhelming.

Is this planet now at the same or similar place? Are we all at a place where we are close to destroying ourselves globally?

Yes, you are. That is why you are sharing my messages.

Some people think they can reach God quicker or deeper, that they will evolve quicker if they abstain from having sex; that there is something advantageous in abstaining from sex. Is this true?

No. Actually, it is the contrary. Humans have a natural desire for sex for a reason. It is not only for the purpose of procreation. Sex expands loving energy, which is spiritual energy. It is an enjoyable and effective 'tool' to expand the movement of spiritual energy. When you expand the movement of spiritual energy, it opens the heart automatically. It helps heal pain in the heart. It promotes love energy flowing through your heart.

When you force yourself to abstain from sex, a great imbalance occurs and it will cause mental delusional thinking. However, if you have guilt and shame, negative judgments about anything, even the most natural and loving acts, it will have a negative effect for you. You are meant to enjoy sex when you naturally desire it. There are times when your desire for sex diminishes. Honor what comes naturally. It is then a time to go inward. Your spirit always guides you. Be aware of it. Honor it. Increase your awareness of your spirit self.

Is it better to be a vegetarian than to eat meat?

It depends on your judgments about it. If you judge eating meat as bad, eating meat will have a negative effect on you. If you honor and appreciate the animal you are eating and do not have feelings of guilt or shame about it, eating meat can actually increase your love and expand your heart. It is all about your feelings. What are you feeling when you eat meat? That will give you your answer.

Some people think that meat has a "lower energy vibration" than plant life. So, they think eating meat lowers their energy vibration, which inhibits spiritual growth. Is this true?

No. It's all about how you feel about it. However, when you eat meat from animals that were treated harmfully, without love and compassion, you are supporting, contributing to the mistreatment of animals. That lack of awareness does need to become recognized. This will bring you forms of pain and suffering to increase your awareness of the lack of love and compassion you have for mistreated animals. If everyone had enough love and compassion for animals, the mistreatment of animals would cease to exist.

When animals are terminally ill and in a certain level of pain and discomfort, near the end of their lives, we euthenize them to save them from more suffering. Is this a good thing?

Yes. As it is now on this planet, unnatural suffering occurs. When they are at the end of their lives and will continue to be in more pain and suffering, it is better to end their lives in a humane way as you do. But, it is a poor excuse for helping. Prevent all suffering by healing yourselves—healing the pain in your heart—spiritually evolving. You are not able to understand how imbalanced you have all become and how you create all dysfunctions on earth. Sickness with animals is also a manifestation of your fear. All suffering is needless.

It seems inhumane that we are not legally allowed to do this [end a suffering life] for our human loved ones and for ourselves

as well. So, for now, with the world as it is, would it be best to do this for humans also?

No. Humans have a different reason for being here than animals. You are meant to live and experience all that you create. Ending your life prematurely will create even more challenging experiences in your next lifetime. Experience what you have created so you can learn what is needed to put an end to all suffering.

That being said, a much easier option is to do Babaji's Work. Prevent yourself from the need to experience trying times for the purpose of healing the pain in your heart. Challenging experiences occur for one reason and one reason only—to help you become aware of your pain and to heal it; to heal your pain, your judgments, your fear. It is only your pain, judgments and fear that keep you in ignorance of knowing who you really are—God.

You can meditate every day of your life. You can try to forgive and love as much as you can. You can do everything recommended in this book to expand spirit. But you will never evolve to your fullest until you feel and then heal the pain in your heart. This is the *only* thing that will free you from your fear. Your fear is the only thing preventing you from being and feeling the full love that you are [God]. There is an easier, quicker way to do this and that is by doing Babaji's Work.

One friend said that regular meditations helped her to automatically remove a fear she had. This was *not* done intentionally by doing Babaji's work. Since regular meditations release stress so effectively, can that process be used instead

of doing Babji's work? It seems easier than to purposefully feel and face our fears.

No. It may seem easier because you are releasing some form of fear ever so gradually, but no. Releasing stress is excellent, it is very helpful. But stress is a *symptom* of your fears. You may feel relief by gradually reducing the symptoms [of your fear], but the fear remains. You may liken this to turning down the volume of a loud noise. Less noise feels relieving and seems better—*and it is better*, but the unwanted sounds still remain in the background. Turning the switch totally off—this is Babaji's Work.

When meditating regularly, you gain momentum by infusing more peace into your being. This process strengthens you and increases your awareness. In fact, it is necessary to become more aware in order to dissolve one's fears; they must first be recognized. Then when the fear is felt (experienced mentally), it can then be accepted, fully healed and removed.

Doing Babaji's Work is a major short cut. Instead of gradual stress release you skip straight to the source—your deepest and worst fears. You confront them head on, face to face. And then they are gone forever.

I will give you an example. Say that you have a fear of the water. Typically when you want to overcome such a fear you may learn to swim as a solution of dealing with the fear. This is not intentionally feeling and facing your fear of the water. Instead, you take baby steps to overcome the fear by gradually walking into the water. Over time, you will walk further going a little deeper, then again deeper still, and so on. Inch by inch you gradually accomplish more.

In time you learn how to stroke your arms, kick your feet, staying near the edge of the pool, or the shoreline, where the safety is. This way you do not feel fearful while you *are* overcoming your fear of the water. You soon become more proficient at swimming. You face your fear of the water by putting your direct attention on gradually learning to swim. This is not such a fearful experience, if at all. But, you have *not* put your direct attention on your fear of the water.

Doing Babaji's Work is facing your fear head on and diving straight into the water. You save yourself the many swimming lessons that really are not necessary. You will overcome your fear of the water in seconds or minutes rather than days, years or lifetimes. Then you face the next fear and the next one, until you reach the deepest one and only fear that is the source of all your other fears, which is the original fear acquired at birth—feeling separation from God.

Some fears require only mild attention, some fears require intense attention to be free of them. Babaji's Work is required for the big, deep ones. Superficial fears are easier to overcome. It is your deeper fears that create the other superficial fears. These need Babaji's Work.

Babaji's Work gets you to that direct fear quickly, quickly, quickly. When you meditate, you do it inch by inch. It's still very helpful, but you can get there quicker now by knowing Babaji's Work. Why do you think you have completely avoided doing Babaji's Work for over two years now Connie? It requires great courage to do Babaji's Work. It is the shortest route, not the long one. Without meditating regularly, it is an even slower, more painful, more uncomfortable route. You are all ready for the quicker route now—removing all your fears that prevent you from having the power of God to become all the Power of YOU. That is why I called Babaji's Work, *A Quicker Path to Christ Consciousness*.

I think our medical system sometimes unnaturally prolongs one's life, facilitating more needless suffering. Can you comment?

I agree. But, experience it anyway. Killing oneself prematurely is no escape from the experience you are trying to escape from.

Now that you brought it up, what is the reason animals are here?

To help you love.

What would you like to say to anyone that is struggling with guilt, shame or regret about something they did or didn't do that hurt someone in some way?

I would tell them to do Babaji's Work. Feel that pain fully and heal it. Give yourself understanding and compassion. Forgive yourself. Nothing good or helpful comes from guilt, shame or regret. Give love to others. Help others heal. Bring a smile to someone's face and heart.

How does someone let go of the resentment, sorrow and disappointment they feel toward their parents? Many feel their parent(s) was the main cause of their inherited bad habits, problems, imbalances or lack of self-worth. Then, they also feel guilt for having these feelings toward their parent.

All pains are healed by doing Babaji's Work. Acknowledge your pain, listen to his mantra to promote the resurfacing of your pain, honor and validate your feelings, feel your pain without judging yourself as wrong or bad for having these feelings, feel the pain as deeply as you can every day until it is gone.

Some people may not be open to any knowledge or guidance from someone that is not of their own religion or culture. What do you suggest if this is an issue for someone?

Do his work and do not call it Babaji's Work.

Connecting the Dots

Danish author, Mette Bergmann, is my dearest and best friend of many years. In her book, *"Missing Pieces of the Soul's Puzzle"* (soon to be translated into English), she recounts a conversation we had with her deceased mother, Edith. What Edith said revealed a much deeper meaning about everything that Jesus and Babaji have been teaching us.

Mette's deceased mother talks about the unknown, underlying source of what caused her own cancer. Edith then recommends how Mette rid herself of her strong fear of flying.

Her example of using one's imagination to face your fears deepened my understanding of Babaji's Work. I had an "Aha" moment. I could now see the real value of Babaji's Work. His process of facing our fears to quickly dissolve them is the fastest way and the only way really, to remove the blocks and obstacles that prevent us from knowing who we really are.

We don't have to acquire God consciousness . . . it is already there. We need only remove the obstacles [fears] that are blocking our awareness of God Consciousness. This can be achieved in one lifetime, many lifetimes or in an instant. As Babaji said, *"it depends on how willing you are to face and feel your pain".*

Our conversation with Mette's deceased mother

[These excerpts from Mette's book were taken out of sequence, so I rearranged them slightly and modified a few words for clarification].

Mette: What exactly created your cancer? Do you know?

Of course I know. The body always responds to your mind's thoughts and feelings. It will copycat them. Whatever you are feeling will manifest inside your body's cells. Emotions will become physical. I worried, worried, worried. I fretted, fretted, fretted and I never really enjoyed what I had. I was too busy feeling fear, feeling lack, feeling there was never enough. The mind will never be at peace, it will never be satisfied. It will always continue to make you feel separate from God and everyone else. As long as you allow your mind to govern your life, you will eventually be in a state of suffering and you will create disease in one form or another.

Mette: Do you remember if all your worries had to do with Claus (Mette's terminally ill brother) or was it many different things you worried about? What did you worry about mostly? What specifically created the cancer in your physical cells?

It was a variety of things, but my son not being well was the straw on the camel's back. I could not bear the thought of my son leaving me (dying) first. I could not bear it; I could not imagine it. It was too painful and I ignored, ignored, ignored. When you ignore the fear in your mind you strengthen it. This creates exactly what you do not want. When you acknowledge and face the fear, it is gone forever. I never had the slightest clue about this. I was just coping. I did not realize that if I faced my fear in my mind, if I said to myself: "if it happens then it happens and I will still be okay", then its power would disappear and the fear would not have been fed and strengthened.

Mette: I have a fear of flying. I somehow got it a few years ago. I guess I am afraid that I could not help Sarika (Mette's 3 year old daughter) if our plane were crashing. What do you recommend is the best way to handle this?

I recommend this: Imagine yourself flying with Sarika and Bent (Mette's husband) and the plane starts to crash. You and her are together holding hands with Bent and looking at each other like you know it is one of your last moments alive and you are helpless and fearful. Imagine you are saying to me: "Mom, I am coming now, it is my time. It is Sarika's time. It is Bent's time. See you in a minute". Then feel that moment of intense fear fully. Make it as real as possible in your imagination. Then walk away and get on with your day. Do this again and again until that fear is overcome.

Question for Jesus:

This advice of imagining what you do not want to happen and doing so with strong feelings, seems like a bad idea. Some spiritual teachers emphasize this practice to create your desires. So, can this in any way create a fearful event to happen at some level?

No. You are releasing that fear by giving it your full attention. It will then be gone forever. Healing your fears is different than trying to manifest a desire. The only reason you are not manifesting a desire in the first place is because of your fears. Without fears, your desires would be fulfilled spontaneously and with no effort.

In Essence of Spirit

Dear reader: I'd like you to know that Mette did follow her mother's advice and she did overcome her fear of flying. This is a perfect example of Babaji's work. It is this simple. Mette was reluctant to picture such a horrifying event yet, she continued the process of visualizing followed by "letting it go" from her mind and then continuing on with her day.

Re: Mette's flying fear:

This is dealing with an obvious phobia (fear). Babaji's Work for most of us includes working to unveil our many unknown fears then facing them courageously and repeatedly until our ultimate fear—separation from God is healed.